S0-AYW-542

The Difference

Also by Jean Chatzky

Make Money, Not Excuses
Pay It Down!
The Ten Commandments of Financial Happiness
Talking Money
The Rich & Famous Money Book

JEAN CHATZKY

The Difference

How Anyone Can
Prosper in Even
the Toughest
Times

 THREE RIVERS PRESS • NEW YORK

Copyright © 2009 by Jean Chatzky

All rights reserved.
Published in the United States by Three Rivers Press, an imprint of the Crown Publishing
Group, a division of Random House, Inc., New York.
www.crownpublishing.com

Three Rivers Press and the Tugboat design are registered trademarks of Random House, Inc.

Originally published in hardcover in the United States by Crown Business, an imprint of the
Crown Publishing Group, a division of Random House, Inc., New York, in 2009.

Library of Congress Cataloging-in-Publication Data
Chatzky, Jean Sherman, 1964–
   The difference / Jean Chatzky.
   1. Saving and investment.   2. Finance, Personal.   I. Title.
   HG4515.C53 2009
   332.024—dc22   2008048881

ISBN 978-0-307-40714-6

Printed in the United States of America

10 9 8 7 6 5 4 3 2 1

First Paperback Edition

For Eliot, who has made a big difference for me

CONTENTS

CONTENTS

ACKNOWLEDGMENTS

I am grateful to so many people for their contributions to *The Difference*:

David Robinson at Duke University was a delightful find and invaluable resource.

Michael Falcon took an interest in this project and brought the resources of Merrill Lynch to the table, including the brain trust of Stephen Mitchell, Vince Grogan, and Aimee DiCamillo; and from Harris Interactive: Humphrey Taylor, Ann Hannon, David Baron, Sonja Anderson, and Carly Fink.

The countless researchers in the fields of behavioral finance and psychology who took the time to walk me through their fascinating projects, including: Angela Duckworth (University of Pennsylvania), Sanjay Srivastava (University of Oregon), Richard Freeman (Harvard University), Wojceich Kopczuk (Columbia University), Sonja Lyubormirsky (Stanford University), Ed Diener (University of Illinois), Robert Brooks (Harvard Medical School), Robert Emmons (University of California, Davis), Frederick Crane (Northeastern College of Business), Katherina Rosqueta (University of Pennsylvania), Dean Keith Simonton (University of California, Davis), Timothy Judge (University of Florida), Charles Manz (University of Massachusetts), Jennifer Crocker (University of Michigan), Barry Swartz (Swarthmore College), Icek Aizen (University of Massachusetts), Edwin Locke (University of Maryland), Robert Meyer (Wharton School of Business), Jay Zagorsky (Ohio State University), Robert

Liden (University of Illinois), Lyle Ungar (University of Pennsylvania), Charles Carver (University of Miami), Alice Isen (Cornell University) and Karen Reivich (University of Pennsylvania), Linda Meccouri (Springfield Technical Community College), Ayelet Fischbach (University of Chicago Graduate School of Business), Daniel Turban, (University of Missouri), Mort Harmatz (University of Massachusetts), Richard Wiseman (University of Hertfordshire), Monica Forret (St. Ambrose University), and Amy Wrzesniewski (Yale University School of Management).

The authors and experts who did likewise, including: Tim Ferris, Seth Godin, Gina Martin, and Doug Harrision.

Jason Zweig—author, expert, friend—who is always so generous with his time and his knowledge.

Monica Roman, Joan Caplin, Elaine Sherman, and Arielle McGowen, for their research assistance.

My Oprah & Friends family: Oprah Winfrey, Harriet Seitler, Tim Bennett, Doug Pattison, Erik Logan, John St. Augustine, Katherine Kelly, Tiffany Square, Charles Gardner, Theresa Rodriguez, Katie Gibson, Katy Davis, and Candi Carter.

My *Today* show family: Matt Lauer, Meredith Viera, Ann Curry, Al Roker, Natalie Morales, Amy Robach, Lester Holt, Jim Bell, Marc Victor, Patricia Luchsinger, Gil Reisfield, Jackie Levin, Rachel DeLima, and all the fabulous producers who help put our segments together.

The people without whom my work life wouldn't be the same: Lesley Jane Seymour, Jennifer Braunschweiger, Craig Matters, Jeff Spangler, Chris Cannon, Erik Kerr, Jason Alderman, Melisa Schilling, Michelle Melville, Rob Densen, Scott Wenger, Wendy Kaufman, Arielle McGowen (again), and Sarah Compo.

And the people without whom my life-life wouldn't be the same: Lisa Greene, Diane Adler, Ilene Miller, Jan Fisher, Debi Fried, Kathy Goldberg, all the Smolers, and my family, Eliot, Eric, Dave, Ali, Elaine.

Heather Jackson, who improves my work with every pass, and the entire team at Crown: Jenny Frost, Tina Constable, Philip Patrick, Tara Gilbride, Karrie Witkin, Patty Berg, Alisha Cantrell, Tricia Wygal, Amy Boorstein, Courtney Snyder, and Linda Kaplan.

Richard Pine, my agent and friend.

Heidi Krupp, who always has my back, and Darren Lisiten, who always has hers.

And, of course, Jake and Julia.

The Difference

What's the Difference?

What's the difference between you and Warren Buffett? Between you and Rachael Ray? What's the difference between you and the guys who launched MySpace or Facebook? Or between you and your boss? Or your boss's boss? What's the difference, for that matter, between you and the success story next door?

I'll tell you what it's not.

It's not that these people were born into money.

It's not that they caught a lucky break.

It's not that they received a windfall like a fat inheritance or a big divorce settlement. Or even that they won the lottery.

It's not that they have an Ivy League education.

And it's not that they are any smarter than you.

It's not even, necessarily, that they earn more money than you each year.

The difference between you and these well-to-do people is not any of the things you suspect it might be.

If you've walked on this planet for any length of time, you've seen what I call "The Difference" work its magic. You've noticed that there are some people who seem to possess an innate ability to rise above any situation. Even during tough times, they effortlessly soar in social settings, at work, and with money. You've seen them and you've wondered: "What do these people have that I don't?"

In high school, they always managed to be at the center of the action, whatever that action happened to be. But not because they were class president or quarterback on the football team. Not because they were better looking or even—in today's vernacular—"mean girls" or "alpha males" who garnered attention and ruled by fear. Theirs was a different sort of magic. Their peers loved them, their parents respected them, even their teachers took extra steps to help them succeed. And, of course, they did exactly that.

At work, they are the leaders—not necessarily bosses, but leaders nonetheless—brimming with confidence that their ideas are the right ideas. They have enough vision to see solutions others don't see, and enough charisma to get colleagues—even those several rungs up the ladder—to buy in. And the people they manage are willing to work really hard to both please them and make them look good. No surprise, they sail up the corporate hierarchy with big fat salary increases all along the way.

And in life? Well, people who fully understand The Difference may have not started out with much, but within a short while, they were richer than they ever expected to be—and not just in financial terms. They knew what they wanted, they plotted a course, and they arrived. They're not stagnant. That wouldn't do. Every day, they think about what's next and set about achieving it with intention and purpose. And today, as a result, they are surrounded by people they care deeply about—and who return the favor. They wake up happy and go to sleep fulfilled. And they don't lose sleep at night worrying about paying that next bill or any other financial matter.

Never was that as apparent as it has been during the difficult financial times that faced this country—indeed, the world—during the past year. As the stock markets took their worst tumble since the Great Depression, as the credit markets ground to a halt, as some banks failed and were eaten up by their flusher rivals, some individuals went into panic mode. Every action was clouded by thoughts of what-if: What if I lose my job? What if my portfolio falls more? What if the price of my house doesn't rebound?

Others were strangely calm. They weren't putting their heads in the sand. They knew just as well as anyone that chaos had consumed the economy. It just hadn't consumed them. That was The Difference at its best.

These individuals knew that they had the information, the habits, the attitudes, and the abilities to not only *survive* in rocky times, but to *thrive* in rocky times. They certainly lost value in their portfolios. They might even have lost a job. But they knew—deep down—that there's more where that came from.

I know what you're thinking. You're thinking where is this Kool-Aid and how can I get my hands on some?

I'll tell you where it is. It's in you. It may be dormant. But you have the power to make the difference in your own life. In fact, you're the *only* one who can. To do it, you'll need to wake up some parts of you that have been sleeping, perhaps for years, perhaps for decades. You'll need to tune in to parts of your personality and tap portions of your potential that you may not have realized you have.

The Difference:
A New Way to Look at Prosperity

I'm sure you've noticed that some people seem to be able to get money with little difficulty. Whether it's the start-up money for a new business, the better salary that comes with a new job or promotion, or the bonus for being the top-selling salesperson, money seems to come to them without a huge amount of strain or stress. They never worry about their finances. They are financially comfortable, wealthy, secure. What do they have that the rest of us do not? What's the difference between you and them?

Thanks to the groundbreaking research conducted for this book, I can tell you—and I can do it in very precise terms. A study of more than five thousand individuals, conducted by Harris Interactive in cooperation with Merrill Lynch, has torn the covers off the four groups of people who make up the new economic strata in America today. They are:

The wealthy (W)
The financially comfortable (FC)
The paycheck-to-paychecks (PTPs)
The further-in-debtors (FIDs)

We now know that the people who have achieved both financial comfort and wealth are distinctly different from those who are struggling paycheck to paycheck or sinking further into debt each month. They are different in their attitudes, behaviors (financial and nonfinancial), personalities, and goals.

The financially comfortable and the wealthy tend to be more passionate about what they do in life, they are more optimistic, and they are more resilient—able to overcome whatever obstacles life throws their way. They are more visionary—able to see things in a slightly different and improved way, if not a new way altogether. They are more connected to others in their professional and personal lives, and they have greater confidence in those relationships, as well as in their lives overall. And they are grateful—incredibly grateful—for the good fortune life has thrown their way.

They are also more likely to come at life with a different mind-set and a different set of skills. They tend to be goal setters who figure out what they want in life and then make a plan to go after it. They are dogged workers (and often need less sleep). The comfortable and wealthy take more risks than the average person, but they listen to their own voices and those of people they trust in order to be as certain as possible that those risks are appropriate for their stage in life or work. And they are always on a quest to learn something new.

The good news: These are all things *you* can learn. Although some people are born with, say, more optimism, it—like every other attribute or skill on this list—can be taught.

And that is what The Difference is all about. The rest of this book is devoted to teaching you how to uncover your nascent talents and develop those abilities. You will discover the latest psychological and academic findings, complete exercises that are easy to incorporate into your everyday life, and read stories of people who've done precisely what you want to do. They've harnessed the power within and used it to reach the same goals you have: financial comfort and long-lasting wealth. Here's a look at what lies ahead.

A Chapter-by-Chapter Breakdown

CHAPTER 1: "Meet the Neighbors." Who are the Ws, the FCs, PTPs, and the FIDs? What qualities and characteristics are moving some ahead, while holding others back? And how can you get a bead on those areas of your life that are lacking and alter your own course?

CHAPTER 2: "Choosing The Difference." This book asks more of you than simply reading it. You're going to go through a series of exercises, tests, and challenges that ask you—essentially—to change the way you actually live your life. If The Difference is going to work for you, there's one thing you need to do first: *Decide* you're going to do it. Choose it. Want it. The fact that you're holding this book in your hands may mean you're already there. But just in case you're not . . .

CHAPTER 3: "Do I Have to Be a Rocket Scientist or a PhD?" No. You don't need to be a straight-A student. You don't have to be a Mensa member, either. But having a college education goes a very long way—and having a lifetime belief that you're never too old to learn something new goes even further.

CHAPTER 4: "Ding, Dong, Your Passion Is Calling." People who know The Difference have figured out what sort of work actually makes sense for them. For them, it's not a job, it's not a career, it's a calling. Once you find yours you'll see it doesn't feel like work—it feels like fun. And once you find it, you won't change course.

CHAPTER 5: "Get Happy (But Not Too Happy)." From the burgeoning study of positive psychology, we now know that optimists—people with a fully formed sense of "subjective well-being"—make more money, scale the career heights, have better relationships, and stay healthier longer. Of course you want to be happy. But perhaps not too happy. Too happy, it turns out, doesn't go hand and hand with wealth.

CHAPTER 6: "In Praise of the Do-Over." What would you do if faced with a difficult—if not dire—opponent? Stare it in the eyes and figure out precisely what you need to do to prevail? Or tuck your tail between your legs and back away? People who have discovered The Difference can and do overcome. In fact, the overcoming itself has made a big difference in them.

CHAPTER 7: "Taking Risks That Make Sense." New work in neuroscience has clued us in to the fact that our brains lead us astray, imploring us to take risks that are, well, too risky, while cautioning us to steer clear of situations that are not as risky as they seem. The wealthy have learned how to evaluate situations astutely in order to take the risks that are appropriate for them. You can as well.

CHAPTER 8: "The Kevin Bacon Principle." You'll never know that your colleague's third cousin once removed sits on the board of a venture fund that has been looking for a start-up just like yours . . . unless you get to know that colleague. Connecting with the world and the people in it—which means putting yourself out there—is key. Growing strong relationships matters.

CHAPTER 9: *"Grazie."* Saying thanks is the ultimate karma kickback. Throw good vibes and gratitude out into the world and both come back to you in spades. The new science of gratitude teaches us that being grateful makes us more successful and wealthier over time. How to say "thank you" is something we can all learn.

CHAPTER 10: "Working Hard *and* Working Smart." There's a train of thought sweeping America that says working hard is no longer necessary. You can do just as well by putting in shorter hours but being smarter about it. Baloney. The Difference points to the fact that you have to work hard *and* smart. You have to want success in your field and apply yourself to get it. It's called "grit." And it's a difference well worth emulating.

CHAPTER 11: "The Healing Power of Saving." Part of The Difference is understanding that spending more than you make is just as bad for you emotionally as it is financially. It certainly won't make you happier. In fact, it does just the opposite. And the worry that comes with financial trouble can quite literally make you sick. Saving money, on the other hand, is actually good for both your health and your wealth. As one noted researcher put it: "Saving money is like healing your soul a little bit every day." The wealthy get that. I'll share their strategies.

CHAPTER 12: "Make Your Money Work for You." You want wealth? Then you need to create an investment plan, take steps to bring it to life, and get help from a financial planner if and when you need it. Our research shows the planning process breeds wealth. I'll show you—step-by-step—what to do.

As you read through these pages, you'll also find a series of boxes on "Habits That Hurt" and "Habits That Help." These feature new research that can supercharge the process of building wealth—or have the reverse effect. The good news is you can control them as well. You will also meet a number of real people who embody The Difference, some so much that it was tough to decide which chapter to put them in. Others have a single standout force that moved them toward wealth. I hope you'll find their stories as inspiring as I do.

A Word About the Exercises in This Book

The exercises you'll find in most chapters will help you master the attributes and habits you need in order to see The Difference in your life. Not every one will be for you—and that's because not every attribute will rank as high on your internal list of what's important. Research has discovered that exercises like these work best when the purpose fits what academics call your "self-concordant motivation." Essentially this means that the purpose is in sync with your values. It's not coming from some internal or external pressure. It's not something that your friends think you should want, or your parents guilted you into thinking you should want. It's something *you* truly want.

I suggest you try every exercise at least a few times. Once is not enough. After a few attempts, you'll get the sense of whether a particular exercise fits. You'll know because it won't feel like work. It may be challenging, but the meaning it brings to your life will encourage you to do it again.

A Final Note

I encourage you to think of the chapters that follow as you might a really delicious meal—or better yet, a tasting menu. You may want to jump from one to the next, because the scallops coming third sound so much better than the tomato salad that's first. Resist the urge. That tomato salad may look boringly simple, but one taste and the flavor of ripe tomatoes hot from the August sun washes over you, sending you back to your childhood garden. Likewise, chapter 12, "Make Your Money Work for You," may sound as if it was written just for you. But if you hustle through chapter 5 on optimism in order to get there, you will have missed some tasty—and powerful—stuff. If you're reading before turning in for the night or hurrying to get to the next section before your train pulls into the station and you have to get to work—stop. Don't do it. The information I'm about to uncover for you is best savored, not bolted. If you move too quickly, you'll rob *The Difference* of some of its power. Roll it around in your mind a bit. Think about how you might incorporate some of the exercises into your daily life. Dwell on the possibilities. Then move to the next course.

CHAPTER ONE

Meet the Neighbors

The New Rich List

Back in the early 1990s, I was—for a short while—a reporter/ researcher for *Forbes* magazine. During my tenure there, I got a few plum assignments, including spending one weekend fact-checking the first interview Michael Milken had granted from prison and fact-checking another on the businessman who would eventually become New York's mayor, Michael Bloomberg. I suppose I did well enough because I was soon tapped to do a little legwork on *Forbes*'s lists of billionaires and richest celebrities.

The preeminent *Forbes* rich list, of course, is the Forbes 400: the list of the country's four hundred wealthiest Americans. It has been around since 1982, when just three families made up 13 percent of the list. There were eleven members of the Hunt family, fourteen Rockefellers, and twenty-eight du Ponts. In 2007, on the list's twenty-fifth anniversary, these dynastic numbers had dwindled to almost nothing. There was one Rockefeller (David Rockefeller, Sr.), one Hunt (Ray Hunt), and no du Ponts. Fifty people fell off the list completely. Forty-five were newcomers—nearly half of whom had made their money in hedge funds and private equity (like Pete Peterson of Blackstone and David Rubenstein of the Carlyle Group); the others

were a mixed bag, including Frank and Lorenzo Fertitta of the Ultimate Fighting Championship, a pay-per-view fight fest.

The point, notes Columbia University researcher Wojciech
Kopczuk, is not just that wealth is less concentrated (the share of
wealth in the hands of the top 1 percent of Americans has fallen by half
over the last eighty years). The real point is that it has moved into a
whole new set of hands. Over the past twenty-five years, as these families have lost their historical positions, a whole new set of people has
gotten rich. Some are entrepreneurs that have made a splash. Others
are high earners on Wall Street, in corporate America, at law firms or
consulting companies. Still others bought the right stocks (or were
handed the right stock options) at particularly opportune times.

This is an incredibly optimistic sign—and it's not just coming
from the pages of *Forbes.* According to the Harrison Group, a research
firm in Connecticut, three-quarters of the wealthy families in this
country—and *nearly all* of those who qualify as upper middle class—
didn't start out wealthy. Eighty-three percent came from the middle
class. They've accumulated wealth over fifteen years on average, which
means that some of them got there in significantly less time than that.
And here's a bonus: When you look at the wealth of the pentamillion-
aires (the folks with $5 million or more), only one-tenth of their money
came from passive investments. They made the rest of it themselves.
Survey after survey I pored over while researching this book shows
that a shrinking percentage of today's wealth came through a bequest.
Research from the Spectrem Group, based in Chicago, found that
only 2 to 4 percent of today's millionaires became rich that most old-
fashioned way. This means you no longer have to be born into wealth.
Despite the hurdles presented by the markets in 2008, the American
dream is alive and thriving—and you have the ability to achieve it.

Where Are Women in This Mix?

The tide for women is turning a bit more slowly—but it is turning,
nonetheless. Remember, there are two ways for people to become

wealthy: They can inherit money or they can earn it. (Some people might argue that marriage is a third proven way to get wealthy. I don't put it on the list because it can also take your financial life in the opposite direction. Nine percent of our survey respondents blamed divorce for a negative turn in their fortunes; 8 percent blamed marriage itself.)

Interestingly, the fact that the ranks of the wealthy are more dominated these days by earned wealth rather than inherited wealth works against women. How? Think about the wealthy American families of yesteryear, the Rockefellers, Vanderbilts, Hearsts, and so on. They had children and their children had children and—on average—those children were likely to be 50 percent male and 50 percent female. So as the money passed from generation to generation, it created as many female millionaires as male ones.

When it comes to earning money, however, men still hold the advantage. Women are making strides. Some 30 to 40 percent of women outearn their spouses. More women than men are entering college and graduate-degree programs. Some researchers predict that the average woman will outearn the average man by the year 2030. But for now, women still lag. In 2007, the number of cents a woman earned for each dollar a man earned jumped from 77—where it had been stuck for as long as I can remember—to 81. Progress, yes, but still not an even playing field.

In terms of wealth and who has it, the number of women inheritors falling out of the ranks of the über-wealthy is—for now—greater than the number of women earners climbing into them. As Columbia's Kopczuk puts it: "Old wealth is split equally. New wealth is not. But as time goes on, we expect to see a more equal split in wealth as well as in income. The tremendous strides women have made in income already indicates we will."

How Do You *Get There?*

This all brings up the questions that are at the heart of this book: Where do *you* fit in now? And how do *you* rise to the top?

I suppose that's fitting, as this entire book unfolded as the result of asking—and attempting to answer—one very large question: Why do some people seem to move relatively easily from a paycheck-to-paycheck existence into comfort or wealth, while others get stuck or—worse—fall back?

I set out to answer that question by reading volumes of research—academic and otherwise—on the subject. Or I should say *subjects:* wealth, education, success, entrepreneurship, risk taking, and the bigger worlds of behavioral finance and positive psychology, which danced in, out, and around the question I was trying to frame. Many professors walked me through their work, explaining their theories and answering my questions.

In the end, though, it wasn't enough. I wanted specifics of which behaviors, attitudes, goals, and personality traits mattered most. I needed to know how these elements *combined* to make The Difference. How many of these behaviors, attitudes, goals, and traits did you need to boost you from one category to another? What, if anything, held you back?

That was when I joined forces with Merrill Lynch and Harris Interactive to develop our own survey instrument that would look—specifically—at these questions. For months, a team of eight to ten of us met regularly. We used the preexisting research as the foundation for our a twenty-minute questionnaire. Then we rewrote those questions, and rewrote them again. Finally, several months later, we administered the poll to more than five thousand individuals.

The Research

The study, formally known as the 2008 Merrill Lynch New Retirement Study, delved specifically into four loosely constructed categories: nonfinancial behaviors, financial attitudes and behaviors, goals (both financial and life), and personality. We asked hundreds of questions about topics including—but not limited to—the following:

FINANCIAL ATTITUDES AND BEHAVIORS: Are you where you want to be financially? Why or why not? What has been the most important factor in reaching your financial status? How do you handle your credit cards? Do you or do you not budget? Do you look up to people with more money than you have? Have you worked with a financial adviser? How do you feel about stocks? Bonds? Do you feel entitled to a good standard of living?

GOALS: What financial goals have been absolutely essential for you as an adult? Save more? Reduce debt? Which goals have you been able to accomplish as an adult? Can you envision a day where you won't have to work to meet your financial needs? Do you see a retirement where you will work part-time? Start your own business?

PERSONALITY: Are you satisfied with your family life? Religious life? Sex life? Financial life? Are you driven to make a lot of money? Are you hardworking? A multitasker? Grateful? Confident? Happy? Optimistic? Stubborn? Creative? Street smart? Outgoing? Competitive? A leader? Ambitious? Popular? A risk taker? Do you have the ability to overcome a bad situation? Are you passionate about your work? Do you finish what you start? Can you easily read other people? Do you feel it is okay to break some rules? Have you compromised your personal principles to succeed professionally?

NONFINANCIAL BEHAVIORS: How many times have you changed occupations as an adult? Do you work more than others? From home? On vacation? How often do you vote? How much television do you watch? How much time do you spend online? How often do you exercise? How often do you read books? Newspapers? Do you participate in extreme sports? Or meditate? How much sleep do you need? How often do you socialize and with whom—friends, family, neighbors, colleagues? People you enjoy? People who could advance your career? Have you made personal sacrifices to climb the ladder of success? Do you give back to your community? Often? As often as you can?

It was a huge undertaking. And that was not all. We asked about political affiliation, left and right handedness, birth order, and whether participants were the children of parents who read to them at night. If we had an inkling that something might be important, we tried to find some way to add it to the soup. And as you'd expect, some of the issues raised by these questions turned out to matter a lot, others not so much, some not at all.

We got the results back in early 2008. But anyone who has ever conducted a large-scale survey knows that the initial data run was just the beginning. For the next half year, the data was processed, cut, interpreted, and reinterpreted. I continued to ask questions. Harris continued to look for the answers. Along the way, David Robinson, associate professor of finance at Duke University—an expert in the field of behavioral finance—volunteered to weigh in. He was insightful and tireless, and with his help, the story in the data revealed itself even more.

The Top Twenty

As noted in the introduction, the research revealed four distinct groups of people: the wealthy, the financially comfortable, the paycheck-to-paychecks, and the further-in-debtors. Unfortunately, the breakdown below reveals that most Americans are still struggling.

THE DIFFERENCE IN AMERICA

	Percentage of Population
The wealthy (W):	3 percent
The financially comfortable (FC):	27 percent
The paycheck-to-paychecks (PTPs):	54 percent
The further-in-debtors (FIDs):	15 percent

What Makes The Difference?

The individuals that fall into these groups vary, of course, in terms of their income and their assets. But these discrepancies in income and assets aren't driving the bus. They're not leading the charge. The individuals in these groups are *fundamentally* different.

As I said, we tested for hundreds of factors. Yet in the end there were twenty factors that rose to the top as key elements. These twenty—literally—make The Difference. Those who "have it" share the following:

FINANCIAL ATTITUDES AND BEHAVIORS
- They feel stocks are worth the risk.
- They devote money to personal savings or a 401(k) each month.
- They save regularly for emergencies.
- They have invested for retirement.
- They have reduced outstanding debt.

GOALS
- They want to be financially comfortable during their working years.
- They aim to retire comfortably.
- They always knew what they wanted to do (for a career).
- They made it a goal to accumulate $1 million.
- They want to own a home.

Personality

- They are confident.
- They are happy.
- They are optimistic.
- They are competitive.
- They are leaders.

Nonfinancial Behaviors

- They have a college degree.
- They socialize with friends at least once a week.
- They exercise at least two to three times a week.
- They read newspapers regularly.
- They are married.

The good news is that you don't need to have all of these factors. The Ws have more of these factors than the FC, who have more than the PTPs, who have more than the FIDs. It's a continuum. But you do need, on average, ten factors (your choice) to make your way into financial comfort—and twelve to make your way to wealth. In contrast, only half of the PTPs and FIDs have more than three of these factors.

The Movers

Finally, working with Duke's David Robinson, I analyzed the data in another way.

Of the five thousand individuals in the sample, there was a significant group who were at one time falling deeper into debt but who have since climbed up into the top two categories. I call these 620 individuals the "movers."

From this analysis, we were able to confirm the importance of the Top Twenty. For example, we saw that individuals who said the word "confident" described them at least "slightly" were significantly more likely to move into comfort or wealth than those who said it did not describe them at all. But we also saw, using this analysis, the emergence of several other important characteristics: gratitude, popularity (connectedness), and the willingness to work hard and take appropriate risks.

We also—quite importantly—learned that several things can hold you back. You won't be surprised to hear that stubbornness is on this list. But how about creativity? Robinson and I spent many hours mulling that one and came away believing it's a particular *type* of creativity that is the problem. It is not conceiving ideas and following through. People who can do that are likely to have said the word "creative" described them "slightly" or "well," and you'll see it helps rather than hurts them. But believing oneself too creative to play in the world of the mundane—these are the people likely to have said "creative" describes them "very well" or "completely"—that is problematic. "If your stubbornness or creativity consumes you," Robinson noted, "those traits become a detriment." Which leads me to a word on moderation.

As you read through these facts and figures, you will no doubt notice that whether we're talking about being happy, hardworking, grateful, or creative, their presence in your makeup is beneficial . . . to a point. If they describe you "slightly," you get a small bump. "Well," a bigger bump. "Very well," the biggest bump. But "completely"? You fall back a bit.

In moderation, all of these attributes are positive and lead to wealth. In full, perhaps not so much. Consider happiness. You'll read more about this in chapter 5, but research has shown that the most blissful individuals don't have enough drive to go for the big job, the big paycheck, the brass ring. They're too satiated, too complacent. That same pattern is mirrored throughout.

As you read through *The Difference,* in particular the profiles of individuals who embody The Difference traits, you'll see that they are—by and large—a balanced group. They are not consumed by one attribute or another but pay attention to many aspects of their lives. They are happy. They are socially connected. They vote. They exercise. They are glowing examples of moderation. I enjoyed spending time with them—and hope you will as well.

Meet the Neighbors

In the next few pages, I want you to meet the neighbors. Read carefully. Your goal is to get a sense of both who you are today and who you want to be tomorrow. Where do you fit? What attitudes and personality traits do you share? What goals and behaviors do you want to adopt?

Where wealth is concerned, individuals aren't stuck in little boxes. You don't start out wealthy, stay wealthy, and end wealthy. Likewise, if you're struggling with debt today, as so many people are, you aren't destined to be there six months or two years from now. These four categories aren't types as much as they are works in progress. People move from paycheck-to-paycheck to financially comfortable, from financially comfortable to wealthy. Sometimes they even fall back, before rebounding to a position of security.

The advice that follows is largely prescriptive. If you'd like to know how to bounce back with the resilience of a person who is financially comfortable, or how to see the glass as three-quarters full like a person who is wealthy, you'll find exercises to help you do just that. Let's take a look at these groups a little more closely—starting with the people you most want to be.

Meet the Wealthy

Confident. Driven. Intuitive. Resilient. Only 3 percent of Americans are truly wealthy. But there is no doubt it's good to be one of them. On average, they have investable assets (not including home equity) of nearly $2 million, but we also categorized them as wealthy if they had achieved significant wealth at a younger age:

- $1 million or more for ages 55 or older
- $750,000 or more for ages 45–54

- $500,000 or more for ages 35–44
- $250,000 or more if under age 35

What made them wealthy? The vast majority didn't get there overnight. Nor did they get there because someone died or handed them a check. In fact, nearly nine out of ten said their wealth developed over time. They credit a combination of the Top Twenty factors for their success. Some are attitudes or attributes that seem to make up their personality; others are habits that support wealth. Both are needed to build a life of lasting wealth. When you have the habits without the personality, you are likely to be financially comfortable, but it's less likely you'll become truly wealthy. When you get the attitudes without the habits, the picture is even less rosy. We have all met that person who is able to get job after job but never climbs the ladder. Without solid financial habits, paycheck-to-paycheck is usually where they get stuck.

Seven Traits of the Wealthy Personality

OPTIMISM. Optimism is an expectation that good things are going to be plentiful. The wealthy generally have the sense that life will bring good rather than bad outcomes. That doesn't mean they believe that good things will be omnipresent, but that they will outnumber the not-so-good.

RESILIENCE. The wealthy are confident in their abilities to overcome bad situations—on the job, in their personal lives, with their finances. Many have triumphed over dismal financial starts. And, unlike most of the population that hops from job to job, career to career, the wealthy are much more likely to stick with what they start.

CONNECTEDNESS. The wealthy are people magnets. They are connected to people in all aspects of life—they have circles of family, friends, colleagues, and acquaintances. One sign of a wealthy person is that others are willing to work for him or her, sometimes for less than they are worth on the open market.

DRIVE. The wealthy want to succeed. Some want that success to arrive in the form of money (and that's OK). But most are quite passionate about the careers they choose to pursue. Not succeeding at these pursuits is, quite frankly, not an option.

CURIOSITY. The wealthy are likely to have gone to college. But it's not just classroom education that sets them apart. They are always learning, consistently reading books for pleasure and newspapers to keep up with the world. This may be a habit learned in childhood; most wealthy individuals report that their parents read to them when they were young.

INTUITION. The wealthy somehow know precisely whom they should be dealing with and whom to walk away from. And they listen to those gut instincts.

CONFIDENCE. When the wealthy take a calculated risk—such as starting a business or buying investment real estate—they don't see it as much of a risk at all.

Four Habits of the Wealthy

WORK HARD. The wealthy work harder—and sleep less—than other people. They are more likely to mix work with their downtime, sacrificing personal time for professional success. But because they tend to be passionate about what they do, it's less likely that they see it as a chore.

SAVE HABITUALLY. Wealthy people certainly have the funds to be crazy spenders, but most are not. In fact, some seven out of ten say that saving more money has been an "absolutely essential" financial goal as an adult. They typically pay off their full credit card balance each month.

INVEST SOUNDLY AND AGGRESSIVELY. The wealthy are more likely to invest in stocks or stock mutual funds. They understand that even in down markets they need to take risks in the market in order to make their money work as hard as they do. They are also more likely to invest in real estate (above and beyond buying their own homes).

GIVE BACK. The wealthy are grateful and they show it by giving back to their communities, to organizations they believe in, and to people they care about.

Interestingly, although the PTPs and FIDs are likely to blame their financial troubles on bad luck, the wealthy say they didn't get there by virtue of a lucky break. They got there by landing a good-paying job and sticking with it. Or by creating, as an entrepreneur, a good paying job for themselves.

It's also important to note that many of the truly wealthy individuals—the millionaires—in our study didn't describe themselves as wealthy. Instead they described themselves as "financially comfortable." Wealth, it still seems, is relative. You're less likely to see yourself as wealthy, even if you live in a huge home on a big plot of land with millions of dollars in the bank, if the neighbors to the left and the right of you have tens of millions in the bank. Likewise, you're less likely to see yourself as wealthy if you run a successful small business, when the other members of your social set run successful midsize ones. Of course, the rest of America—and most of the world—indeed views you as wealthy.

With wealth, you get a greater degree of contentment with the other aspects of your life. Although study after study has shown that wealth in and of itself can't buy you real happiness or inner peace (and my own research noted that people who believe it can are less satisfied with their lives as a result), as you climb the ladder of financial success, you do become more satisfied with many parts of your existence: your family life, social life, health, religious life, even your sex life.

WHAT DO THE NEIGHBORS THINK?

Are you extremely satisfied with your sex life?

	Yes
Wealthy	37 percent
Financially comfortable	30 percent
Paycheck-to-paychecks	21 percent
Further-in-debtors	16 percent

Now, who wouldn't want a little piece of that?

Meet the Financially Comfortable

Like the wealthy, the 27 percent of Americans who are financially comfortable are standing on solid—well above average—financial ground. On average, they have investable assets of $240,000—a number that rises with age.

Their good habits have put them there. The financially comfortable are even more likely than wealthy individuals to make—and stick to—a budget. In other words, they're careful about how much they spend. They're similarly careful about how much they borrow. Nearly 70 percent pay off their credit cards in full every month, and the rest either pay more than the minimum or don't use cards at all. Three-quarters devote a chunk of household income each month to personal savings. That's striking in an America that for the last decade has been saving nothing at all.

These are people who, like the wealthy, are in a good place—not just financially but in life. In large part, money does not stress them out. A scant 2 percent—a number so small it could be a result of statistical error—say money causes headaches in their lives. Only a handful say they'd have any trouble whatsoever paying a large medical bill if it hit unexpectedly, or staying afloat if they lost their household income temporarily. Although they're not *as* satisfied with their social lives, health, or sex lives as the wealthy are, they're just as satisfied with their family life, which makes sense, since they are more likely to be family focused, but less so on friends, colleagues, or neighbors.

With all of those positives, why haven't the financially comfortable become wealthy? They're missing a few solid pieces of the wealthy personality. They're less optimistic. Less likely to take a risk at an advantageous time. Less likely to reach out of that inner, familial circle to make a connection with someone who holds the keys to getting ahead. As a result, they are a little less grateful as well.

Don't get me wrong. Financially comfortable is not a bad place to be. It's a place most Americans should aspire to. But once you reach it, digging into your soul and unlocking The Difference will allow you to reach heights—in wealth, success, and happiness—that perhaps you never realized were possible.

Meet the Paycheck-to-Paychecks

A life where you can buy what you need but never what you want. Where after paying for housing, food, and clothing, you have very little left to pay for anything else. Where gas-price hikes make you ask: "What do I have to give up today to put enough in the tank to make it back and forth to work?"

This is reality for more than half of all Americans. More than half! Some 54 percent say they're stretching it, living from one paycheck to the next. They're making ends meet, but they're struggling to do it. Any unexpected expenditure could tip the balance in the wrong direction. A large medical bill. A hole in the roof. And it's taking a toll. One-third say their financial situation is causing a lot of stress in their lives.

Why are they here? What separates the paycheck-to-paychecks from the financially comfortable and the wealthy? Both personality and habits. But in this case, the habits are the driver. Sure, sometimes the catalyst is something out of your control, such as a health problem or job loss. But our research showed that overspending is *the key reason* that people slip from a position of financial security into a paycheck-to-paycheck existence. Consider how many people are on precarious ground because they bought houses they couldn't afford to live in or maintain. How many are on shaky territory because they bought one too many pricey cars, took yet another expensive vacation, or fashioned an image fueled by wearing the right clothes, eating in the right restaurants, or walking the right dog?

It's a vicious cycle. Once you overspend, it's tough—if not impossible—to tap into the habits that move people into the range of the financially comfortable. Once you overspend, you cannot save habitually. Credit card debt is a savings killer, and only 22 percent of paycheck-to-paychecks can pay off their balances every month.

But while overspending doesn't leave much to invest, it doesn't leave zero. More than one-third of these people participate regularly in their company's 401(k) or some other retirement plan. This automatic investing is clearly responsible for the somewhat surprising fact that paycheck-to-paychecks have investable assets, on average, of $83,000. If the number sounds higher than you'd expect, that's because it's skewed by what I like to call the "six-figure PTPs." These are the high earners—the managers, lawyers, entrepreneurs—who still can't seem to make ends meet. The folks who feel broke despite the fact that they're bringing in $100,000-plus a year. Fully half of paycheck-to-paychecks, however, have less than $25,000 to put to work to grow their futures.

Being in this position does not inspire confidence. Or happiness, resilience, risk taking, gratitude, or any of the other attributes of the wealthy personality. Even when they do have assets to invest, they're not investing them the way you must to become wealthy: aggressively enough to beat taxes and inflation. Three-quarters say the stock market feels too risky for them. One-third can't even envision a day when they won't have to work to meet their financial needs.

Again, this is not a life sentence. If you're in a paycheck-to-paycheck position, learning—and then practicing—optimism, resilience, appropriate goal setting, and prudent risk taking will put you in position to find your passion in life. Once you find that passion, you'll no longer feel the need to overspend to fill the emptiness in your soul. In fact, because you're more self-satisfied, you'll be inspired to take care of yourself in other ways by saving more, investing appropriately, and annihilating that credit card debt. Likewise, saving more, building up that retirement account balance, investing it for growth, and watching the balances on your monthly credit card statements dwindle will put a smile on your face and make you feel you can conquer the world.

Meet the Further-in-Debtors

Finally, there are those people who can't even tread water. They're already in a hole, but instead of making their way out, they're tunneling down further. Some 15 percent of Americans say they're sinking further into debt each month.

It's a dire picture. Less than one-quarter of further-in-debtors save anything each month or make a contribution to a retirement plan such as a 401(k), which is why 56 percent of them have less than $10,000 in investable assets to their name. Three-quarters say if they had a large medical bill tomorrow, they would find it difficult to pay. Not surprisingly, they're both unhappy and insecure. Nearly half get physical symptoms like insomnia, heartburn, stomachaches, or headaches when they think about their finances.

What do they blame for their situation? Bad luck.

What do I blame? Hubris.

The paycheck-to-paychecks overspend and know they're doing something that's not in their own best interest. The further-in-debtors overspend without a thought because they feel entitled. They deserve the nights out, the new clothes, the latest technology. How do I know? Our research gave me a peek into their budgets. A full third devote a decent chunk of their budget to entertainment or extras—nonessentials as far as I'm concerned. Far fewer devote any money at all to saving for tomorrow.

Can they change? Can they turn the situation around? Absolutely.

They need to embrace as many of the components that make up The Difference as they can. And they'll need to use the arsenal of tools in the chapters that follow to keep themselves on the right track.

Moving On Up

In my last book, *Make Money, Not Excuses,* I wrote about an epiphany I had—a good fifteen years into my finance career—when I realized there are only four things standing in the way of any one individual and financial security.

1. You have to make a decent living.

2. You have to spend less than you make.

3. You have to invest the money you're not spending so that it can work just as hard for you as you are working for yourself.

4. You have to protect yourself and this financial life you're building so that a disaster—large or small—can't come along and take it all away from you.

I am absolutely right on these four points. Absolutely. Positively. Without a doubt.

But what I have also come to realize is that these four steps are a bit of an unbalanced equation. There are two sides to living any financial life. The left and the right sides of the ledger. The assets and the liabilities. The money coming in and the money going out. Numbers 2, 3, and 4 are all about the money going out.

Spending less than you make? Most people in this country are not. We have been, for the last two decades, living on a diet supplemented (if not on paper, then at least with a little mental accounting) by the fat values of our tech-laden stock portfolios and then, when those petered out, with the rising values of our four-bedroom Colonials. As a result, Americans have been saving an anemic one-half of 1 percent of everything we earn. That's eight times less than the percentage of our income we spend every year eating out. Yet, it is fairly simple to right your ship by tracking your spending, cutting out needless expenditures (big and small), and reducing the interest rates you're paying on your debts.

Investing the money you don't spend? That's not something most of us are doing sufficiently, either. First, of course, you have to find the money. Then you have to deal with a convoluted system of accounts ranging from 401(k)s to IRAs to Keoghs to SEPs, figuring out which is the right one for you and how to fill it with the right mix of stocks and bonds once you open it. But again, this is a situation fairly easily remedied with a series of automatic monthly transfers from paychecks into retirement accounts, from bank accounts into 529 plans, from checking into savings. And once the money's there, if you don't care to spend your time picking stocks, you don't have to. Find a target-date retirement fund (sometimes called a lifecycle fund) geared to the date you plan to stop working full-time and call it a day.

Protecting everything you've built? Strike three. To this day, two-thirds of Americans don't have the most basic of legal documents: a will. Or enough life insurance to take care of the people they love, should something unforeseen happen. But, again, this can be remedied relatively quickly and inexpensively. (Term life insurance prices have gotten so competitive, I just replaced my five-year-old policy with a new one and am saving hundreds of dollars a year.)

What sets numbers 2, 3, and 4 apart is that although you may be fully capable of mastering these skills—and you may have one or more of them under control—they are things you can do sufficiently only after you have taken care of number 1—that is, after you have the money rolling in. And therein, as the Bard would say, lies the rub. Try as hard as you like to follow my advice—and I've been told I make understanding how to accomplish 2, 3, and 4 very easy—to track your spending, save automatically, and reduce your outstanding debt. Try to allocate your assets to perfection and pick winning stocks or mutual funds with low expense ratios. Try to secure your future with the right amount of term life insurance coupled with a well-rounded estate plan, a will, durable powers of attorney, and health-care proxies. Try all of this, but if you don't have the money—and you can't figure out a way to get the money—you are going to fail.

A Swiftly Shifting Paradigm

The good news, the very good news, is that this is a situation that can change—and quickly. Ten years ago, one in ten of the people who today describe themselves as financially comfortable were slipping further into debt each month, and four in ten were living paycheck to paycheck. In other words, half of the financially comfortable made their way not only out—but up. Ten years ago, 16 percent of the individuals who today describe themselves as wealthy were mired in debt. Only 13 percent were wealthy back then, which means that for a full 87 percent of them—nearly nine out of ten—wealth has been a recent phenomenon.

And it doesn't always take ten years to make the leap. Those individuals who transitioned from living paycheck to paycheck into a life that's financially comfortable said it took an average of seven to eight years. Moving from financially comfortable to a life of wealth took just over eight on average. And making the big leap—from paycheck to paycheck to wealth itself—took about ten. That's the number of years *Friends* spent on the air. It's about the same time that a successful president spends in the White House. It's equivalent to the career life span of an NFL running back. In the scheme of things, it's a blink of an eye. And most people—no matter what strata they're living in right now—believe making that leap is possible. Are you one of them? Read on.

Your Choice

What do you need to do to find The Difference in your own life? Two things. First, you have to make the decision that this is a course you are going to embrace. You have to choose The Difference, just like you choose to exercise, eat healthier, quit smoking, read nightly to your kids. You choose The Difference; it does not choose you. The power is in your hands.

And once you choose it, you need to do something. I recently had a long and inspiring conversation with Don Green, who, for the last decade, has run the Napoleon Hill Foundation. I asked him what separated Napoleon Hill's fine work—most notably *Think and Grow Rich*—from latter-day works on the law of attraction. He told me that Napoleon Hill believed that first you had to see what you wanted; you had to envision the good things to believe you could actually accomplish them. If you were not able to even see them in your own mind, then you would project to the world an attitude of no confidence, desperation, failure—and failure would then be inevitable. But Napoleon Hill also believed, and this is what set him apart, that once you saw those good things, then you had to take specific actions to make them a part of your reality.

I agree.

The Difference is as much about doing as it is about believing. It's about making your own luck, not taking no for an answer, and paying attention to the things you're doing—both right and wrong—so that you can accomplish more with fewer sidesteps in the future. Believing alone won't make it happen. All the wishful thinking you can muster won't make it happen. *Doing* makes all the difference in the world.

A Quick Guide to Chapter 2

Deciding to find The Difference is the first choice you'll need to make on this journey—but it is not the only one. In this chapter, you'll learn how to set concrete goals, to break them down into manageable pieces, and to deal with the fact that reaching them in the long term almost always means overcoming some short-term obstacles. You'll also see how your stubbornness—and, believe it or not, creativity—can stand in your way.

An Aside

This is the first of many times the chapters in this book bleed into one another. In just a moment, you'll meet Jerry, and you'll see he has many of the important differences. A large number of the people you'll meet will. And that's because having one helps you develop others, which helps you develop others still. The differences circle one another, diving in and out, weaving a nice little web that becomes a life. They rarely work independently.

The work we're doing here is just one example. The point of this chapter is to help you use tools and information to set and reach your goals and make The Difference a part of your life. But as you move on to the next chapters, you'll start to see the connections. Setting and reaching your goals provides a big boost to self-esteem, helps you overcome obstacles, and aids in figuring out which risks make sense to take.

But those same things also help you set and reach your goals.

Take that self-esteem connection. Timothy Judge, a management professor at the University of Florida, studied life insurance agents and found that people with what he called "high core self-evaluations"—healthy self-esteem or a high opinion of themselves—set more aggressive sales goals, were more committed to those goals, and when faced with initial failure persisted in trying to reach those goals longer than agents with lower self-esteem. His other research suggests that people who believe in themselves seek out more challenging jobs (if you don't believe you can do it, why would you even try?), which leads to greater salaries down the line.

The point: This is not one of those books you'll likely read and put down. Dog-ear the pages of the exercises that make the most sense to you. Flag pages with abandon. Write in the margins, start a Difference Journal, or pick up the companion we've published with this book. As you learn things in later pages that make you recall something from an earlier chapter, flip back (this is why we include an index) and read it or try it again.

MEET JERRY

AGE: Fifty-four
FAMILY: Married, two children
ASSETS: $1 million to $2.5 million
JERRY'S DIFFERENCES: Resilient, takes risks, grateful, hard-working, wealth is a goal

There are some people who are born with every advantage in the world. There are others who have to make their own way. Jerry is one of the latter. He wasn't handed anything. But he was driven to make a better life for himself than the one his parents had. And he succeeded, because he knows The Difference.

Q: Tell me about your background.

A: I grew up in the '50s and '60s in the Park Slope neighborhood in Brooklyn. I came from a hard-knocks family, a tough environment. My mom and dad were working and barely making ends meet, but they still managed to provide for us. My dad was blue collar and Mom was a stay-at-home mom. She worked part-time in clerical and retail jobs.

I went to a Catholic high school and college, and I footed my own bills through college. I started as a premed over at St. John's, but decided to switch my third year. I wasn't hacking it, so I switched into civil engineering. I did very well my third and fourth years and got into a decent grad school. Again, I put myself through.

Q: Then what happened?

A: After grad school, I started working for the city. Then I was called to a civil engineering consulting job and I moved to work for the federal government, the EPA. On the side, I decided to investigate Wall Street. I was always intrigued by Wall Street.

Q: So you caught the stock bug. Did your interest in the stock market coincide with the beginning of the bull market in 1982?

A: Actually, I started to trade for my own account in the '70s. My first stock was Lockheed Martin, and I did quite well. I started very small to get my feet wet. And then I decided in the early 1980s that I wanted to work as a stockbroker. I passed the Series 7 Exam [allowing him to sell securities] in the early '80s. At that point, I had my own stock and bond account. But I decided to take it further, to pursue a part-time career after my regular job, and I started servicing other accounts.

Q: How did you find your clients?

A: I started with friends and family, but over time my customers were strangers. At that point I worked part-time for various firms on Wall Street. It's tough to get into the big brokerage firms of the world part-time. I ended up at fly-by-night bucket shops that were pushing penny stocks, but I didn't get wrapped up in their philosophy. I learned as I went along. I watched how principals operated, and I tried to figure out what my course should be.

Q: You were still working full-time as an engineer while you were doing this?

A: Yes, but I really got involved in Wall Street. I got as involved as I could. In the '80s, I took the Series 24 Exam, which allows you to operate a brokerage firm. That was a big deal for me. I opened a brokerage firm with a lawyer and back-office gentleman in Chinatown. It imploded because one of the parties got greedy. Lost a half million by hooking up with a promoter from Florida. Here was my dream to leave the engineering business, but it didn't work out that way.

Q: What did you learn from that experience?

A: As far as the loss sustained at the brokerage firm, and the short life of my dream business, I vowed I would never get involved in another partnership or take a chance on someone who is less than honest. I certainly was humbled by that experience. There are no shortcuts in life, but I bounced back with vigor! I still had my government job to fall back on (it paid the bills, although it left me with little extra discretionary income). Even though we failed miserably, I surmised it would only be a short period of time before I would come up with a new plan to create wealth. I was still young and hungry to succeed.

Q: And since then?

A: Since then, I don't take risks I can't afford. I take calculated risks. In stocks, I'm a fundamentalist. I look for companies that have some value. I tend to stay with companies in basic industries. And I look for conservative PEs [price/earnings ratios].

My philosophy has always been to take a long-term approach. If you do your homework up front, you don't get burned. And sometimes you take a loss when a loss is due. I purchased a stock recently—MoneyGram International—at $4.20. Within maybe twenty minutes of purchasing the security, bad news about the stock comes out and it's down to $3.80 a half hour after I bought it. It turned out they might have exposure to subprime loans. It was time to make a decision. I sold the stock.

Q: What are your basic rules of investing?

A: I never buy stocks that have long-term debt or negative equity. I never chase stocks. I try to avoid stocks that are making new highs. It's fair to say I share Warren Buffett's philosophy. My goals are shorter-term than his. I try to purchase a security and be out of the position in a year. I'm very happy taking small gains.

Many times I purchased a stock where the market was trending lower but the fundamentals were good. Markets go up, markets go down. If you pick good companies, you don't get caught up in that. I put together key statistics and run my own screens, but I'm not going to tell you all my secrets. It's very simple analysis.

Q: How about your gut? Do you follow it?

A: Gut instinct is a factor as far as the entry point. But exiting a stock is a totally different story. That's when you put emotions aside. It's easier for me to buy a stock than to sell. If you made money on a trade, so be it. But don't look back.

Q: So, you're on Wall Street full-time now?

A: No, I never left the environmental field. I work as an engineer to this day.

Q: What has driven you to have two careers all these years?

A: Well, my inner drive to create wealth was my own, and still is, even today! My incentive was "never to be without money in my wallet," which I had experienced through the early years of my life. I vowed never to be worried about where my next dollar would come from.

Look, I started with zero. But I have the energy to set a goal and then get where I want to be. It's pure drive that sets me apart.

CHAPTER TWO

Choosing The Difference

There's a scene toward the end of the movie *The American President* where Michael Douglas—playing President Andrew Shepherd, a widower with a young daughter, who has recently entered into a romantic relationship for the first time since losing his wife—strides into the press room. He is quite clearly on a mission. He has been holding his tongue for three-quarters of the film as the opponent standing in the way of his reelection, Senator Bob Rumson (Richard Dreyfuss, at his snarky best), criticizes his character—and the character of his girlfriend.

A reporter asks the press secretary, "Is the president going to answer Senator Rumson's question about being a member of the American Civil Liberties Union?"

In—to everyone's surprise—comes Shepherd, who says, "Yes, he will." He asks the press to take their seats. And then he proceeds to speak.

"For the last couple of months, Senator Rumson has suggested that being president of this country was to a certain extent about character. . . . I've been here three years and three days and I can tell you, being president of this country is entirely about character."

Shepherd continues, defending his membership in the ACLU before moving on to defend his girlfriend.

"America isn't easy. America is advanced citizenship. You've gotta want it bad, 'cause it's gonna put up a fight."

The speech goes on from there. It will go down as one of writer Aaron Sorkin's very best, just after the "You Can't Handle the Truth" diatribe from *A Few Good Men,* and just before the "Two Cathedrals" episodes (a two-parter) from *West Wing.* I bring it up because The Difference is very much like Sorkin's America.

The Difference isn't easy. The Difference is an advanced concept. And yes, you have to want it, because it will—in all likelihood—occasionally put up a fight. It is, in that way, like the marathon you want to run. The diet you want to undertake. The smoking you want to stop. And the money you want to save. The Difference is a choice that you make each day.

Ambition: The Wanting Is Paramount

A few years ago, I was on *The Oprah Winfrey Show* for a five-part series called "The Debt Diet." After we shot the first show and introduced America to the three families who would be undertaking the challenge of getting out of debt on national television, Oprah said, "Let's do an after-show." She had more she wanted to say on this subject and she opened it up to questions from the studio audience.

A young woman in a red dress stood up and started running through all the reasons she didn't think "The Debt Diet" would work for her. She needed to go out to eat with her friends. She needed to refresh her wardrobe. She needed to buy shoes. Oprah looked at her and said simply: "You're not ready."

Precisely.

But let's assume *you* are not the woman in the red dress. You are not Bob Rumson. You are ready. You not only want it, you want it bad. In other words, you are ambitious. This is key.

Look at our movers—those individuals who were living paycheck to paycheck or getting further in debt who are now financially comfortable or wealthy. When we asked them if the word "ambitious" described them, it was clear that relating to that word even a small amount was crucial to getting out.

Attribute	Describes Me	Percent More Likely to Move Forward Than Those Who Said the Word Didn't Describe Them at All
Ambitious	Slightly	18 percent
	Well	15 percent
	Very well	17 percent
	Completely	13 percent

"In other words," said Duke's David Robinson, "ambition is almost a necessity."

Why is complete ambition not as good as a lot? Moderation is rearing its head. If you are too focused on getting ahead you may not learn what you need to along the way. You may also irritate someone who has the power to bring (or keep) you down.

So you've got the desire. You've got the ambition. How do you get yourself to make a commitment to—and then stick with—the tenets of The Difference? Icek Aizen, a psychology professor at the University of Massachusetts, has studied precisely that: the psychology of action. How do you get yourself to do something that you want to do?

On its face, it seems to be a no-brainer of a question. If you want to do it, why wouldn't you—as the Nike commercials say—just do it? Because, as Aizen explains, even goals that seem on the surface to be 100 percent positive have negative elements embedded. The long-term benefits you reap are at war with the shorter term compromises you have to make.

When Goals Collide

Take a simple example. What if you want to lose a few pounds? In fact, let's say you've actually articulated that as one of your goals. But what if you also want to eat food that tastes good? You have two separate goals that seem to be in direct competition with each other. (Let's forget for a second that some wonder-cooks can whip up healthy, low-calorie food that actually tastes quite delicious. In my forty-some years of eating experience, the more butter and sugar an item contains, the more likely it is to put a smile on my face.)

Look at starting an exercise program. The positive result of getting up and out a few times each week to take a spinning class, lift weights, or run a few miles is long-term good health. In the short term, however, it's time-consuming and—particularly as you're scaling the learning curve of coordination and stamina—not at all fun. That's why America's gyms are crowded in January on the heels of New Year's resolutions and empty by mid-March.

Or consider the goal of saving more money. You can believe with your entire being that saving money is a good thing in the long term, and that what experts like me say about your financial future hinging on your own savings (rather than a corporate pension or Social Security) is absolutely, 100 percent true. But in the immediate future, the fact that you're putting away your money rather than spending it has not-so-desirable consequences. It may mean you can't eat out as often. Or that you have to wash the car yourself. The fact that the positives come years down the road—putting your kids through college with a minimum of loans or enjoying a lush retirement—doesn't help matters. Voilà: our nation's problem with credit card debt.

So what do you do in the oh-so-many situations where one goal that offers the ultimate prize but requires some delayed gratification loses when squaring off against a lesser goal (Chocolate! Sleep! Shoes!) that happens to be available immediately? How can you satisfy all your goals? Or at least prevent the quest for one to sabotage your chances of achieving the others? You do it by performing what the psychological community calls a "hedonic calculus." You likely already know this—

and how it works—by its street name: a back-of-the-envelope or legal-pad analysis. Essentially, you make a list of the things you want and put them in order. Which are crucial? Which can wait? Which, in the scheme of things, don't matter much at all? Do you keep postponing the real goal until it never becomes a reality at all?

Then you reach for balance. It's imperative to build smaller rewards—treats in the case of a diet, small purchases in the case of saving for a larger goal—into the program so that you're not "cheating." You're doing what you must to stick with the plan. Say your main goal is a flourishing career. Your side goal is frequent vacations. How do you do both at the same time? By scheduling your business trips on a Thursday and Friday and spending Saturday in the sun or at the hotel spa. You may spend a few dollars on a hotel room for the night, but your company picks up the airfare. Get the idea?

Watch yourself—monitor your behavior—to optimize your results. What happens if you indulge first? Is your follow-up better or worse? If you schedule the pleasure trip on a Sunday, followed by Monday and Tuesday on the clock, does that work better than working first and kicking back later? Or on the plane home on Tuesday do you feel like you didn't have a vacation at all, and therefore call in sick on Wednesday?

There are things that you can do to help yourself with this quest. These aren't principles that are restricted to absorbing The Difference. They'll help you stick to any new program and achieve any goal you set for yourself. They'll also help you make the changes the rest of this book will ask you to consider.

Here's how to turn complicated goals into realities.

Distinguish Goals from Fantasies

At a recent reception, a friend of a friend described her hoped-for future. "I'm fifty-two and burned out. I've been working in the same industry, in one job or another, for the last thirty years. I'm tired of the commute. I'm bored with what I'm doing. And so I've been thinking about quitting and starting my own business doing college counseling.

There are so many high school kids around here who could use a hand figuring out which schools to apply to and how to fine-tune their applications. And I think I could do pretty well, financially."

Fantasy? Or goal? That is completely up to her.

We all have fantasies in our lives. They're things that we want and often express to others.

"I want to change jobs."
"I want a second child."
"I want to save more money."
"I want to be happier."
"I want to retire."

Those of you who've been listening closely to me on the *Today* show or on the radio have likely heard me utter mine more than once:

"I want to buy a beach house."

Fantasies all, and fantasies they will remain until we break them down and figure out (a) what is standing between the place where we are now and the place where we have acquired those things or made those accomplishments, and (b) if we are willing to make the sacrifices necessary to get from here to there.

Even positive goals require sacrifice. Changing jobs requires sacrificing free time to update your résumé, network, and interview. It means being willing to bear the unease that comes with starting again as the new kid, whether you're the new kid in the cubicle or the new kid in the corner office. Retiring may sound like a picnic, but it means sacrificing the pleasurable twenty minutes you spend each day with colleagues—by this time, more like family—talking about nothing in particular. It means forgoing the sanity that comes in the form of a paycheck, as you run the calculators to make your nest egg last as long as you do. Even my beloved imaginary beach house comes with the downside of knowing that I'd be racked with worry the next time a hurricane was on the way.

Goals also require that you sacrifice time. Many of them—retirement, raising children, attaining happiness that's lasting rather than fleeting, growing wealth—are not one-time events. You can't simply check these things off your list. Rather, they will take years. They may take decades. And in the meantime, you'll have all sorts of other goals you want to pursue.

What Makes a Goal Achievable?

How do you know when your goals are right for you? How do you know when they're actually achievable? Researchers conducting experiments on these questions have asked people to make predictions, such as when they will finish a paper. They find that good goals are generally somewhat optimistic but not completely unrealistic. This is key. For your goal—whether it's one you've set for yourself or one someone else has set for you—to be one that you can realize, it has to have four distinct qualities.

BUY-IN. A goal, like The Difference, doesn't work unless you're ready. You have to want it. It's as simple as that.

ACHIEVABILITY. If you are working for an employer who sets a "stretch" goal for you—20 percent more sales this year than you made last year—that stretch goal can give you a mark to reach for, but only if you believe you can do it. Likewise, even if you want to run a marathon, you won't cross that finish line if you don't believe you have the stuff. In that case, you're better off stretching for a half marathon or 10K.

POSITIVE IMPACT. A goal is more achievable—and researchers have found you'll be more committed to it—if its overall impact on your life will be positive. You have to be able to envision that life later, after the goal is reached, the weight is lost, the bank account balanced. And that life has to look better. If you're one of those people who believe that if you look too good in a swimsuit or become too rich your friends will desert you, chances are you won't be able to hit those goals.

COMPLEXITY. Interestingly, goals are easier to reach if they're complex rather than simple. If reaching a goal is too easy, then in your mind, you don't accomplish anything by getting there. It becomes devalued because of its simplicity. If, on the other hand, a goal seems too complex—if the number of steps between you and the finish line is confounding—then to be successful you need to break that goal down into smaller components called "benchmarks."

Goals Versus Benchmarks: Why You Need to Break 'Em Down

Once you have a goal that seems to have these four characteristics, then it's time to chunk it out. You wouldn't get in the car and, lacking GPS, drive straight from New York City to Poughkeepsie if you hadn't done it before. First, you'd grab a road map or go to the computer and download some directions.

Think about your goal as if it were a set of MapQuest directions. Each time you're supposed to make a left or a right, or merge onto the parkway, you pause, you think, you act. Those are benchmarks. You know, thanks to MapQuest, approximately how long each step will take you, how much distance you'll travel on the way, and if you should be looking for any helpful landmarks.

What if you find that your particular goal is hard to map and monitor? Chances are, it's not well defined. Your goal might be "I want to be successful in my career." Well, what does that mean? A promotion every eighteen months or tacit approval from your supervisor that you're doing a good job? Either one is fine, but you can't meet specific goals until you define their specific parameters. So decide "I want to get a promotion eighteen months from now, and another eighteen months after that." Then start mapping precisely what you're going to have to do to make that happen.

One Goal at a Time

Have you ever wondered why college students tend to gain weight during exam period? Because, it turns out, humans are the sort of animal with mental resources best focused on a single goal at a time.

An Op-Ed that ran in the *New York Times* on April 2, 2008, under the headline "Tighten Your Belt, Strengthen Your Mind" made that point precisely. It discussed recent research that found that people who successfully handle one goal requiring willpower—such as losing weight or exercising—have less success if they simultaneously take on a second task requiring willpower.

"The brain has a limited capacity for self-regulation, so exerting willpower in one area often leads to backsliding in others. The good news, however, is that practice increases willpower capacity, so that in the long run, buying less now may improve our ability to achieve our future goals—like losing those 10 pounds we gained when we weren't out shopping," wrote authors Sandra Aamodt and Sam Wang.

So what do you do to avoid being held back by this fact?

Short term: Decide what the most important goal for the short term is and use your willpower to accomplish it without allowing yourself to get sidetracked. Even things you might not believe take willpower often do. The *Times* story specifically suggested not window-shopping for items you can't afford on your way to a party where you don't want to over-imbibe. The window-shopping could drain you of your willpower. Similarly, if you need all your energy to study for a big test, you might be best off letting other willpower-needing activities (exercise, dieting) slide.

Long term: It's harder to set priorities when you're dealing in a time frame longer than a few days, but that's precisely what you have to do. You have to decide whether it's more important to you to go on that one-time vacation or to put away $2,000. These are questions that can be tough to answer. The fact that you want many things simultaneously makes it difficult to allow one to float to the top. These strategies can help.

Fact: Some Goals Are Better Than Others

The headline above sounds like a value judgment. It's not. The thing that makes some goals better than others is not the what, but the why. It's not what you're reaching for, it's why you want it.

University of Michigan psychologist Jennifer Crocker has studied what she calls "inside goals" and "outside goals." Inside goals are those things you want for yourself. Outside goals are those that contribute to something larger. The latter is preferable.

Why? Because when life becomes a competition, nobody wins. People who are focused only on themselves and what they want for themselves tend to have a zero-sum version of their relationships with other people: If you get it, other people don't. If other people get it, you don't. Everything becomes a contest—you win or you lose— which creates an environment of fear, confusion, ambivalence, and conflict. Life in this scenario becomes a pressure cooker. And in the end, the goal to escape the pressure cooker overtakes whatever goal you set initially.

Take a student whose primary aim is to appear smart or competent. He's not trying to learn; he just wants to look like he's learned more than others. In and of itself, this is anxiety provoking and undermines the student's ability to be focused. Because he's never able to figure out where the bar is set (will the guy at the next desk sound even smarter or more competent?), this student procrastinates, doesn't get things done, and doesn't make progress.

On the other hand, people who focus outside of themselves, setting goals that are more constructive and collaborative, often feel calm, connected, and clear. These positive emotions help keep the most important goals at the forefront and encourage getting things done rather than procrastinating.

Take that same student, but this time his aim is to make friends. This is not—as you might think—a wrongheaded goal for college; popularity is a predictor of success and wealth, which we'll see in chapter 8. This sudent is always there to help his roommate who is struggling in biology, and is repaid when the chemistry midterm is weighing on his own mind. He and his classmates want to see one another do well, reach their life goals, and succeed—and the fact that they are there for one another is indicative of the likelihood that they will do just that.

When Wealth Is the Goal

When the goal is wealth—money; riches; cold, hard cash—the parameters are exactly the same as they are for any other goal. Society wouldn't have you believe that. Society, aided by certain religions, has drummed it into our heads that wanting wealth is a bad thing, an unhealthy thing, one that will drive you to behave in ways that are unethical, corrupt, and morally bankrupt.

I disagree. In large part, wanting wealth seems to be key to achieving it. Our research shows that people who stated wealth as an important goal are much more likely to achieve it.

"Accumulating a million dollars or more has been an absolutely essential financial goal for me as an adult."

	Percent That Agreed
Wealthy	45 percent
Financially comfortable	11 percent
Paycheck-to-paychecks	8 percent
Further-in-Debtors	6 percent

The primary issue is not whether you want wealth. The primary issue is *why* you want it. What is your motivation for wanting to create wealth?

Earlier research taught us that money means different things to different people. From my own Roper study of money and happiness, we know that three-quarters of people believe money means security.

Two-thirds believe it means independence and comfort. And one-third of people believe that money means happiness. (That last one-third is in trouble. More on them, momentarily.) Those different meanings reside in our consciousnesses and our souls, and drive our quest for more money.

If we are reaching for wealth because we want to provide stability for our families or the families of those people who work for us, that is acceptable. If wealth is a by-product of creating a business we are passionate about, or working hard and doing well at something we truly love (be it opening a restaurant or running a hedge fund), that is perfectly fine. If we have goals of making the world a better place by adding something we believe will be valuable, that is a healthy motive. We are, in all those instances, giving more than we are getting.

What is not so healthy? Wealth as a yardstick. A measuring tool. A means to impress others or to prove our parents wrong. Wealth that we want to prove we're better than others. In other words, wealth desired for getting, not giving.

Wanting wealth in that context is not only unhealthy—it will make you miserable. You'll be in a constant state of anxiety or doubt. University of Maryland leadership professor Edwin Locke told me this story: In Virginia, a man he knew built a huge house on a street that was home to many wealthy people, some of them multimillionaires. The man loved his house. He equipped it with the best appliances, top-of-the-line finishes, and every amenity you can imagine. A few years later, a neighbor bought an empty piece of property and built a bigger house. The first man couldn't take it. He tore his down and started over.

It's sad. Pathetic actually. More so, because it's absolutely true. Say you want a painting for your wall. Do you buy one that's famous so you can say to your friends, "I have a Monet"? Or do you buy one you love based on your own personal judgment and preference? One that puts a smile on your face every time you pass it and sends you out into the world a happier person. By now you know the difference.

Watch Out!
Traps That Will Get in Your Way

As you're reaching for any benchmark or goal, there will be a time that your resolve begins to slip. Chances are, this will happen for one of two reasons.

The first is the "What the Hell?" effect. Say you have been working to save more money for what seems like ages. In reality, it may have been only twelve weeks. But trust me, it will seem like much longer than that. You zip onto the Web, log in to your online savings account into which you have made monthly transfers of cash—three now. And you will see that you have . . . $606.36. And you say to yourself: "This is nothing. It's not enough for a new TV. It's not enough for a vacation. I am not getting anywhere. What the hell, I might as well just spend it."

The second is the "I Deserve It" effect. In a similar example, you will have been working to save money for what seems like ages. You took your $2,400 tax refund, used that as a starter cushion, and have been adding to it to the tune of $200 a month for the last three months. You have $3,000, plus interest. And you're feeling great. So great, in fact, that you buy a $1,500 new computer on a whim. You tell yourself you deserve it because you've been doing so well saving money—not even realizing that you just cut your savings in half.

Excuses, both, says Ayelet Fischbach of the University of Chicago Graduate School of Business. People see initial resistance as an excuse to get out before "wasting" any additional effort. Similarly, they see initial success or partial progress as an excuse to disengage from their goals. The key is knowing how long it will likely take you to reach your goal, and then mapping that progress. Her suggestion: Think about the benchmarks you hit as a way to measure your commitment. Opening a savings account or increasing the amount of your monthly transfers become signs that you're going to save more money—not signs that your goal is already attained.

HABITS THAT HURT: KEEPING UP WITH THE JONESES

If you're spending everything you make and more, you are sabotaging your ability to reach your financial goals. You know this already, right? So why are Americans such a disaster in this area? Blame your brain. In neuroscience labs at academic institutions across the country, brains are being hooked up to MRIs to see what makes them excited, and therefore what drives impulsivity and what doesn't. Instant gratification is driving the bus.

Our brains are much more enticed by the notion of money today than getting some tomorrow. Offer the money months into the future and our brains couldn't care less. Even if the amount we're offered next week is slightly bigger than the amount we are offered today, it doesn't matter. We want it now. This makes it very difficult to save for tomorrow. And when we get emotional about it—and who doesn't get emotional about a shiny new iPhone or a stunning pair of shoes?—we fare even less well. The future reward has to be truly substantial to get us to walk away.

So, what to do? Simply knowing that this is how you're programmed can help you stave off your hoarding instincts. In addition, you can employ a few mind games to get yourself going.

AUTOMATE, AUTOMATE, AUTOMATE. The nice thing about automatic saving is that you have to do something only once and the money can roll in forever. Call your bank and elect to have money moved every month from checking to savings. Call your benefits manager and increase the contribution to your 401(k) or—if your company offers it—opt for automatic escalation, which will bump up your contribution every year. Go to the website for your college savings plan of choice and have money swept automatically into a 529.

PICTURE IT. What are you saving for? You not only need to be able to describe it but to see it. You know the house in your town that you can't drive by without thinking "Someday . . . "? Take a snapshot of it. Then make it your screen saver. Put it on your fridge. Shrink it and tuck it into your wallet (preferably right next to the credit card). And while you're at it, attach a date to that dream, so that in your mind you're not only living in that four-bedroom Cotswold, you're living in that four-bedroom Cotswold on July 23, 2013.

> TELL SOMEONE. Find a friend or a spouse to be a cheerleader to help you overcome your natural urges and get you to this goal. If you're feeling your resistance start to wane, this person becomes the go-to guy or gal whose job it is to talk you out of doing something impulsive.

Exercise: Map Your Goals

Now you're ready to put all of the tools in this chapter together and map your way to a successful goal. You can do this on paper or on your computer. Either way, seeing your goals formed into actual words helps emphasize their seriousness. Here's the outline to follow and then an example to refer to for inspiration.

THE GOAL:
What do you want?

THE RATIONALE:
Why do you want this?

TOTAL ANTICIPATED TIME COMMITMENT:

EXPECTATIONS
- How will you feel when you reach this goal?
- What impact will reaching it have on your life?

HURDLES
- What do you expect will get in your way of achieving this goal?
- What sacrifices do you expect you will have to make to reach it?

The Benchmarks

1.

ANTICIPATED TIME COMMITMENT:
EXPECTATIONS/HURDLES:

2.

ANTICIPATED TIME COMMITMENT:

EXPECTATIONS/HURDLES:

HURDLES:

3,

ANTICIPATED TIME COMMITMENT:

EXPECTATIONS/HURDLES:

And so on . . .

Example

THE GOAL: Get a master's degree in education.

THE RATIONALE: Earn a better salary; better positioning for jobs in school administration.

TOTAL ANTICIPATED TIME COMMITMENT: Two to three years, on a part-time basis.

EXPECTATIONS

- How will you feel when you reach this goal? Satisfied that I have crossed this off my list. More confident in applying for new positions.
- What impact will reaching it have on your life? Greater financial security.

HURDLES

- What do you expect will get in your way of achieving this goal? Life. With two kids and a job, getting to class will not be easy.
- What sacrifices do you expect you will have to make to reach it? Time with my friends and time with my spouse will likely both be cut short. I may have to get up an hour before the kids—or stay up an hour later than my spouse—in order to study.

The Benchmarks

1. FIND SEVERAL SUITABLE PROGRAMS NEARBY AND GET APPLICATIONS.

ANTICIPATED TIME COMMITMENT: One month.

EXPECTATIONS/HURDLES: This shouldn't be difficult, I should be able to get recommendations from friends and from online research.

2: APPLY TO PROGRAMS.

ANTICIPATED TIME COMMITMENT: One month.

EXPECTATIONS/HURDLES: I estimate I can fill out one application per week. Getting letters of recommendation will require me to start talking to people about what I'm doing.

3: APPLY FOR FINANCIAL AID/SCHOLARSHIPS.

ANTICIPATED TIME COMMITMENT: Two weeks.

EXPECTATIONS/HURDLES: I'll have to go online and get the FAFSA. It would be very nice to be able to pay for this without going into massive debt. I'm going to search the scholarship databases to see if there are any grants available for people with my skill set, and I'll talk to the financial aid officers at the schools I'm applying to about what they would recommend.

And so on . . .

You see, there may be many benchmarks along the road to meeting your ultimate goal. The more, in many cases, the better. They keep you honest and centered so that you—and everyone you've rallied around you—knows where you stand.

A Quick Guide to Chapter 3

Intelligence and education. The assumption of the masses is that most of the wealthy in this country have both—at very high levels. And yet, that's not what the research bears out. In this chapter, you'll learn that when it comes to The Difference, street smarts matter as much as book smarts, and education is important—but it certainly doesn't all have to happen in the classroom. We'll also discuss how to find a mentor and why it's truly beneficial. And you'll discover what to do if you're given a candle, a box of tacks, and some matches and told to attach the candle to the wall so it doesn't drip on the floor when lit—and what it says about the way you think.

MEET FRED

AGE: Sixty-eight
FAMILY: Divorced, six children
ASSETS: $1 million to $2.5 million
FRED'S DIFFERENCES: Takes risks, flexible, always learning, able to read other people, resilient

When Fred was a young boy, he would sit around the kitchen table with his father and have conversations that went something like this:
Father: You're going to college.
Fred: No, I want to be a policeman like you.
Father: No. [Getting angry] You're going to college.
Fred: No . . .

Fred's father passed away when Fred was still in high school, but he'd be proud to know that not only did his son become a policeman, he also got that education. Only he did it in a way that was decidedly his own. As Fred says today, "There are a lot of college-educated morons in my opinion, but I don't think I'm one of those. College set my brain in a direction that I wasn't interested in prior to that time."

Q: Why the opposition to college?

A: In high school, my grades were average to below average. I was a good boy, participated in every sport. But academia was not a huge ambition of mine. So, rather than go to college, I went into the military. And I'm not exactly sure what happened—I hope this doesn't sound pretentious—but some intellectual curiosity bit me. I thought, "I want to try this out." Once I started, I liked it. I kept going and going.

Q: Where did you go to college?

A: Indiana University after the military—I must have been about twenty-one or twenty-two years old. Then came marriage and a move to California, and then the L.A. Police Department. I ended up going to a couple of community colleges and then a state institution, and eventually I got my master's.

Q: What do you think compelled you?

A: I'm one of those people who get bored easily. I can't do the same thing over and over.

Q: I have to imagine that when you were first married, a young policeman, you weren't making much money.

A: You're right. My wife was a schoolteacher, so she wasn't making much money, either. It wasn't hand to mouth. But could we buy anything we wanted? No. In fact, I remember when we first started out I bought a brown booklet kind of folder that I marked "entertainment," "food," "mortgage." I'd get my paycheck and put a certain number of dollars in each slot. I remember putting $15 in entertainment and it had to last two weeks. But it didn't bother me.

Q: Why not?

A: I'm going to tell you a story. I don't know if I can do it without getting choked up. When I was a young sergeant, in 1968 or '69, I worked down in south-central L.A. I was working in uniform, getting ready to get off, when there was a huge house fire. The house was not in a good part of town. There were four children in the house. It was the police department's job to help out the fire department. So after the fire is out, I go in because they still hadn't found the children. It turns out the mother had gone out drinking and left her four kids. I remember pulling out one of the dressers and finding one of the kids behind it dead. All four of the kids are dead.

Now it's over and I get in the car and I'm driving home. As I get closer and closer to my home I'm driving faster and faster. A couple of blocks from the house, I literally visualize my house on fire. I come around the curve and . . . it's not. I park the car, go straight into the kids' bedrooms, and I kiss each one. Then I get into my bed, kiss my wife on the cheek, and I try to go to sleep. I did eventually.

I realized two things that night: I needed to spend more time with my children, which meant not climbing the ladder on the force. And that I needed to make a lot more money so that I could help my children go to college and start their lives.

Q: That's a pretty tall order, particularly at that time and particularly—and I don't mean to be sexist—for a man. Spend more time with your children. And get rich? How did you do it?

A: Almost by accident. We were going to have our third child. We needed a bigger house. We found a nice home, that was the stimulus. So I held on to the first one and rented it out. My friends said, "Suppose you have trouble finding renters?" I think it was a time when maybe people in my social structure weren't doing that, but I just saw the opportunity. Why sell it when I could keep it and rent it and make income from it? To me, it wasn't risky. It was a tax write-off and it was simple arithmetic.

[He laughs.] My wife said to me years later, "You're not a risk taker." I thought to myself, "Don't you know me? I've always taken risks." At the police department I always took risks—I was lucky I was never killed. As an undercover, I took risks. Young men think they are infallible and invincible. To me, it came naturally.

Q: After you caught the bug, did you layer one property on top of another?

A: It took a while. After fifteen years of marriage, my wife wanted to divorce me. I was still madly in love with her, we had six children. I was devastated. But I wanted the kids in the house—it was a nice house. So I took the rental property. Eventually I sold it and used the money to buy a few multifamily units. I moved into one and I would rent the others. Sometimes I'd sell within six months for $50,000 or $60,000 profit, which was a lot back then.

Q: What was your secret?

A: Discipline. The first place I bought had a nice home sitting in the front of the property, and it had two units behind. To get to the secondary units, you had to go through an alley. I remember thinking I could rent out the house for a lot of money, and that I would live in one of the duplexes in the back. I know how to live without having to be showy.

The place needed fixing up. I put in a fence, plants, did some nice things. Not even a year later, I sold it and made a hell of a profit. Then I moved into a five-family unit, and bought another in between. Location is important. Being able to fix it up is important. But the real bottom line is this: Do the numbers work? I hear people say, "I'll buy a piece of property as long as it pays for itself." Not me. It can't just pay for itself. It has to make a profit to be worth my time.

Eventually, I wanted a nicer place to live in myself, so I sold almost everything. My real estate broker said, "Why are you doing this? You're on the road to being a multimillionaire." I said, "I don't care. I need a different kind of stability in my life."

Q: What did you do with the money from your real estate investments?

A: I bought mutual funds and stocks. I did my own research. I'd take the Sunday paper, take a couple of hours and look at the mutual funds—all of them. I'd take a red pencil and mark those making 30 percent or more. Then I researched them some more to see if it was a fluke. I'd look at the three-, five-, and ten-year performance histories, and I always invested in no-load mutual funds because anyone investing in load mutual funds is crazy.

One year, on just three mutual funds I made 33 percent, 58 percent, and 82 percent. That was almost unheard of. But to me, it was common sense, research. The key is not when to get into it. It's when to get out. Most people, when they start to lose, they want to stay in, stay in. That doesn't always work.

Q: And you stopped investing in real estate altogether? Why?

A: Fast forward to today: I'm retired from the police department. I have a nice pension and investments. I teach one night a week. I have freedom, health, personal enjoyment of life—these were all more important to me than more money. Would I say that if I were struggling now? No, but I'm not.

You and I are having this conversation, but I can't say this to 99 percent of the people around. I don't need the money; I don't need it practically and emotionally. I'm smart enough, emotionally, to realize that I could have a hell of a lot more. But why? I have a nice home, a couple of nice cars, wonderful children. I'm satiated.

Q: Could you have achieved what you did without your education?

Academia gave me a certain level of self-esteem and self-confidence. People are very reluctant to say that. When I teach now, students are a captive audience, and I digress sometimes. I say, "I don't want to meet you on the street and hear you say you got a highfalutin' degree. I want you to go on, not just for money but for self-respect and knowledge." I've had students come up to me after finals and say how it encouraged them.

CHAPTER THREE

Do I Have to Be a Rocket Scientist or a PhD?

No. You do not. Just like Fred did not. That's the short answer. But that is not to say that intelligence and education—the two attributes people most associate with earning a lot of money and achieving wealth—don't fit into this picture. They do—one more than the other. Thankfully, the one you can control is the one that really matters.

Let's start with intelligence. For years, many people assumed that smarts—most specifically IQ—played a significant role in determining financial success. New research shows this is not the case. In 2007, Jay Zagorsky, a research scientist at Ohio State University, used data from the U.S. Bureau of Labor Statistics to prove this point.

Zagorsky used data on 7,403 randomly selected young baby boomers that the BLS had been tracking and interviewing repeatedly (to date, twenty-one times) since 1979. He defined wealth as I do here: the difference between a person's assets and liabilities; in other words, how much money someone would have to rely on in the event of an emergency or a longer life event such as retirement. He defined financial difficulty as a "situation where [someone's] credit is adversely impacted, such as not paying bills or charging a credit card to the maximum limit." In other words, a definition that adheres very closely to the paycheck-to-paychecks and further-in-debtors I looked at in my research.

Among the individuals in Zagorsky's research who are now in their early to midforties, he found that although there was a link between intelligence and income (the top 2 percent of society based on IQ alone is earning, on average, $6,000 to $18,500 more a year than someone with a normal or average IQ), there was no link between intelligence and wealth. No link, as he puts it, between brain power and earning power. In fact, in what may be a statistical anomoly (but one of those fun facts reporters like me love to grasp on to), subjects who had an IQ of 105 had the same median income as those with an IQ of 110, but they had net worth that was 17 percent higher.

Those findings, of course, raise a few questions:

- What are all of those supersmart high earners doing with that extra income if they're not turning it into wealth?
- Why wouldn't they be smart enough to put something away for tomorrow?
- Isn't that the very definition of "smart"?

Zagorsky surmises there's overconfidence at work. These very intelligent folks might believe they can bank on their brain power to earn them sizable paychecks tomorrow—so they feel free to spend everything they have today. They may have let that overconfidence talk them into buying bigger houses, pricier cars, and overconsuming in general, which can impede the building of lasting wealth. My personal belief is that these smart and well-compensated folks may also be struggling with student debt from years in pricey colleges or graduate schools. (Interestingly, the top-of-their-class students who take the "calculus" track rather than the "basic math" one are less likely to get financial education as part of their curriculum. But as they're more likely to attend better—and often more expensive—colleges and universities, and rack up thousands of dollars of debt in student loans, you could argue that they need it even more.)

That's why I wasn't surprised to see that being very smart doesn't protect you from financial hardship. People all along the IQ spectrum max out their credit cards, declare bankruptcy, and miss bill payments.

On the whole, these findings are positive. Essentially, you don't have to be an Albert Einstein, Isaac Newton, or even your run-of-the-mill genius to attain financial comfort or wealth in America. What you do need is an education. Preferably a college one.

School Rules

The data on education is clear and conclusive. Every level of education you complete dramatically increases your shot at greater income and, in turn, greater wealth. Individuals who complete high school earn more than those who don't. (There are very few millionaires who didn't finish high school.) Those who complete some college courses earn sizably more than those who simply graduate from high school. And those who complete college take a big jump in earnings over those who simply start it.

AVERAGE INCOME BY EDUCATION		
	1995	2004
No high school diploma	$25,800	$25,900
High school diploma	$43,000	$44,800
Some college	$49,900	$56,000
College degree	$87,900	$117,500

Source: U.S. Federal Reserve, Survey of Consumer Finances, 2004

The income discrepancies are largely due to the salaries individuals with or without college degrees attract. In 2007, for example, the average hourly wage for someone in manufacturing was $17.35. In professional and business services, wages were three dollars higher, $20.59 on average. And information technology paid nearly four dollars better still, $24.11. The difference between the manufacturing wage and the latter two, economists explain, is the rate at which they grow. Manufacturing wage inflation lags even the rate of inflation.

Those extra earnings translate into additional savings. That makes sense; the more money you earn, the more you should be able to sock away for the future.

PERCENTAGE OF FAMILIES THAT SAVE MONEY BY INCOME GROUP

Less than $20,000	34.0 percent
$20,000–$39,900	43.5 percent
$40,000–$59,900	54.4 percent
$60,000–$79,900	69.3 percent
$80,000–$89,900	77.8 percent
$90,000–$100,000	80.6 percent

Source: U.S. Federal Reserve, Survey of Consumer Finances, 2004

And with that jump in income comes a jump in net worth. The net worth of an average family headed by a college graduate is four times the size of one headed by a person whose education ended with high school. Four times.

Education not only helps you start earning money, it helps you keep earning it, as recent unemployment data proves. In November 2008, the unemployment rate for people who had not finished high school was 10.5 percent, for those with some college (or an associate's degree) it was 5.3 percent; and with a bachelor's degree, it fell to 3.0 percent. In times of rising unemployment, these differences become more important.

AVERAGE FAMILY NET WORTH BY EDUCATION OF
HEAD OF HOUSEHOLD

	2004
No high school diploma	$136,500
High school diploma	$196,800
Some college	$308,600
College degree	$851,300

Source: U.S. Federal Reserve, Survey of Consumer Finances, 2004

In the future, having an education will be even more important, because not having one will set you apart—and not in a good way. Some 20 percent of baby boomers earned a college degree. Nearly 40 percent of their children—Generation Y—have a college education, and that number is increasing. Not only will the lack of a degree put you behind, but today's jobs demand special, often college-taught, skills. For more than forty years we've been losing manufacturing jobs in this country. That trend continues today. We are shedding the lower paying, labor-intensive jobs and adding higher paying information-intensive ones.

College Is Key to Staying Debt-Free

Of the individuals who say they're going further and further into debt each month, a full 42 percent had no education beyond high school. That number fell with each increase in wealth. Likewise, with education came wealth. Sixty-four percent of wealthy individuals had completed college and/or gone beyond it; only 22 percent of further-in-debtors had.

WHAT IS THE HIGHEST LEVEL OF EDUCATION YOU'VE RECEIVED?			
	High School or Less	Some College/ Associate's Degree	College or Graduate Degree
Further-in-debtors	42 percent	36 percent	22 percent
Paycheck-to-paychecks	39 percent	31 percent	30 percent
Financially comfortable	27 percent	26 percent	47 percent
Wealthy	10 percent	25 percent	64 percent

Graduate school makes an even bigger difference, it seems. Although research from the federal government doesn't track the wealth of people who extend their education beyond college, perhaps it should. Forty percent of our wealthy respondents had completed graduate school. That was also true of 17 percent of the financially comfortable, but only 8 percent of the paycheck-to-paycheck responders, and just 5 percent of those sinking deeper into debt.

The moral: Get an education. As much of a classroom education as you can. But perhaps even more important . . . don't stop there.

Learning Every Day

When people meet me, they inevitably want to know a couple of things: Did I major in business as an undergrad? And where did I get my MBA? I tell them no, I majored in English as an undergrad (that always gets a laugh). And as for the MBA, I don't have one. I am—for the record—the least educated person in my immediate family. My father had a master's and a PhD; my mother has a master's.

Do I regret the decision not to continue my education? Not really. I continue to learn every day.

As I said earlier, in the early 1990s, I was a reporter at *Forbes* magazine. Getting that job was one of the toughest challenges I had faced in my life up to that point, but I was determined to do it. I had started my career at *Working Woman* magazine. It no longer exists, but in its 1980s heyday, it was a quirky amalgam of business and fashion, food and glass-ceiling stories. I was the assistant to the business editor and got to write short profiles on companies like Gap and Nike. In doing so, I fell for business journalism—and I fell for it hard.

At *Working Woman,* I had a colleague named Walecia Konrad— we all called her Wally—who had started her career as a reporter/ researcher at *Forbes* magazine. This glorified title was given to the fact-checkers, who repeated the reporting done by more seasoned writers and reporters to be sure no mistakes made it into print. Wally said this was the best job on the planet. You worked, she said, until two in the morning. You were yelled at on a regular basis. On a really bad day, nasty comments about some of your work might make it into a public computer file where everyone could read them. And yet, if you wanted to be a business reporter—a really good business reporter—there was no better training ground in the world. And so I was desperate to go to *Forbes.*

The problem? *Forbes* wasn't so desperate to have me. I finagled an interview with the chief of reporters, who sat me down and intoned, "I have a stack of résumés a foot high . . . and you're here." He gestured to the bottom. I was blown away.

"What do I have to do to get a job here?" I managed to ask.

"Go get an MBA," he replied.

Well, I had enjoyed college plenty. But I knew that grad school wasn't for me. I wanted to be in the business of earning money, not spending $40,000 a year on tuition. Particularly to land a job that would pay me half that. So I waffled for a little while. I did some free-lancing for other business magazines. I spent some time in cooking school, thinking that perhaps I could get myself excited about writing recipes or reviews. And still, I was desperate to one day walk—as an employee—into that classic Forbes building at Twelfth and Fifth, where Fabergé eggs held court in the lobby and Steve Forbes called each and every employee on their birthday.

And then it dawned on me that the chief of reporters wasn't telling me to get an MBA specifically. He was telling me to get MBA-like skills. To learn to read a balance sheet, to dissect the financials of a company, to be able to ask intelligent questions of a CEO. That, I knew, was precisely what stock research analysts did every day. I figured one of those analysts might find it handy to have someone writerly around to help write those research reports. So I started applying for jobs on Wall Street, and quickly landed two.

I went to work as an assistant to three research analysts in the health-care department of what was then Dean Witter Reynolds on the sixty-third floor of Tower Two of the World Trade Center. I had access journalists didn't get—at least not in those days—to CFOs, COOs, and CEOs. I visited company headquarters and learned the intimate details of patent protection for pharmaceuticals—and why it matters. One day I traveled to Atlanta to witness one of the very early laparoscopic gall bladder removals—a procedure that would revolutionize surgery and send the stock of a company called U.S. Surgical soaring. And, yes, I learned how to pull apart those financial documents.

I learned every day. I enjoyed learning so much that part of me wanted to stay. In the end, though, I couldn't let go of the dream. And so, two years later, I reapplied to *Forbes*. When I sat down in front of that same chief of reporters, he said the same thing, "I have a stack of résumés a foot high." This time, though, mine was at the top. I had a job in two weeks. And in that job—as in every other I've held since— one of the things I look for is a constant, continuous ability to learn.

The wealthy do precisely the same thing. They have a commitment to continue learning—again, not necessarily in a classroom. They are more likely to ask a question than to answer one, and they are more likely not to be satisfied with that answer until it makes sense.

> *"I read newspapers at least five times a week."*
>
> | | Percent That Agreed |
> | --- | --- |
> | Wealthy | 66 percent |
> | Financially comfortable | 53 percent |
> | Paycheck-to-paychecks | 33 percent |
> | Further-in-debtors | 28 percent |

Street Smart and Book Smart

I was going to call this section "Reading Is Fundamental" because if you're anything like me, you remember those RIF ads from when you were younger. You know which ones I mean—they involved a traveling library and free books for kids. But as I took another look at the research, it became apparent that street smarts are equally important to book smarts. What are street smarts? They're a certain sort of savvy. The sort that allows you to read people and prevents you from being taken advantage of or scammed. That tells you to turn right when right just happens to be the correct way to go and left might land you in the boonies. Just 40 percent of the total population say street smarts are part of their genetic makeup, but 51 percent of the wealthy say they are. Likewise, just 27 percent of all people surveyed say they can "easily read other people"; 42 percent of the wealthy do.

HABITS THAT HELP: READING FOR FUN

Of course, being book smart is important as well. A 2007 report from the National Endowment for the Arts, which was based on an analysis of two dozen other studies, found that when students do not have sufficient access to books, their performance—as measured in test scores—slips, not just in language arts but in other subjects such as math and science as well. School isn't the only environment where people are falling behind and subsequently suffering. Employers are reporting that many of their workers lack basic writing skills.

"I read books for pleasure."

	Percent That Agreed
Wealthy	64 percent
Financially comfortable	59 percent
Paycheck-to-paychecks	50 percent
Further-in-debtors	47 percent

The lesson: Read—and encourage your children to read. And if you can, make sure that they live in a house with books (or make time to visit the local library). The NEA study looked at the average 2005 math scores of twelfth-grade students who lived in homes with fewer than 10 books compared with those who live in a house with 100-plus books. It found that those in the homes with 100-plus books scored much higher. That you might expect. Then they looked at the same scores of students in households with 100-plus books in which the parents had completed only high school, compared with students in 10-book house-holds in which the parents had completed college. Again, the students from the households with 100-plus books prevailed. An emphasis on learning something every day—particularly by reading—cannot be discounted.

Find a Mentor

There are other ways to learn, even if you're not in school. One is to attach yourself to a mentor—a person higher up in your company or industry who can serve as a role model and provide the counseling, friendship, honest feedback, and direct assistance that can help you get ahead. Studies show that people who receive mentoring throughout their careers draw higher salaries, receive more promotions, and are more satisfied overall with their life's work than those who do not.

Spend any time in the workforce, though, and you'll notice that some people find mentors, but others don't. How do you make yourself one of the chosen?

That's a question researchers have only recently started to ask, explains Daniel Turban, the chair of the Department of Management at the University of Missouri Robert J. Trulaske Sr. School of Business. One of his areas of specialty is organizational change. There is a risk to mentors if they choose a protégé who does not succeed, he says. It reflects poorly on the mentor's judgment. So mentors look for people who not only appear competent, but tend to be motivated at work.

The people who receive more mentoring also tend to be more extroverted and outgoing and have greater emotional stability—they take on challenging situations and handle them confidently and appropriately. In fact, appropriateness turns out to be important in and of itself. Turban's research shows that those people who get the most mentoring have the ability to read social cues well and to tailor their behavior to a particular situation—in other words, they're not likely to embarrass their mentor at the company Christmas party.

In your search for a mentor, keep in mind that mentors gravitate toward protégés with whom they have something in common, such as social status, upbringing, or someone who reminds them of a younger version of themselves. Research has shown that mentoring is most effective in same-sex, same-race relationships, which may make it more challenging for minorities to find the best mentors.

Interestingly, though, the most important factor in finding a mentor may be the willingness to look for one: Mentors tend to select people who seek them out. If you're looking for a mentor, you'll need to take the initiative, start a conversation, build a relationship, and ask for what you want.

Pick someone who is highly respected, suggests Turban. Say hello a couple of times. Then ask him or her: "I'm wondering if we can get together for coffee or lunch—I'd like to get some advice." You can even preface it by saying that you know they're well respected and busy, and you'll be careful of their time. Don't come out and say, "Will you be my mentor?" but something more along the lines of "I'm wondering if I can stop by from time to time with questions?" Think of it as dating. You can go on lots of dates, but you may never come right out and ask that person to be your Valentine. Things just progress or they don't. The same is true here.

And while you're reaching out, you may want to multiply your efforts. The traditional view of mentoring is that you should find one person to help you along the way. Newer research suggests that having multiple mentors is a better way to go. Why? Because just like no one friend can usually fill all your needs—the guy you grab a few beers with on a Friday night may not be the same one you'd invite to a documentary or have an intense conversation with—no one mentor may be able to help with all your work and life challenges.

Finally, you may also want to become a mentor yourself. We usually think of these as one-way relationships. But, in fact, mentors benefit, too. Protégés, who are typically younger, tend to have more up-to-date technical expertise. They can help an older mentor adjust to newer technologies. Mentors also see a boost in their reputation if one or more of their protégés succeeds. But the biggest benefit, by far, is the psychic boost you get from giving back. Paying it forward by helping someone reach their goals feels good. It feeds the soul.

Thinking "Flexibly" Helps, Too

You're probably familiar with the term "creative thinking." Well, Alice Isen, professor of psychology and S. C. Johnson professor of marketing at Cornell University, doesn't like it. It invokes a sort of loopy genius, she explains. The type of person who can figure his way through one complicated brainteaser after another but can't get to the office because he forgets to put gas in the car.

Thinking flexibly—which is, despite Isen's word preferences, a form of creative thinking—is not like that at all. It is not crazy or wild. It's just the opposite—very organized. It's the ability to turn things around in different ways, look at various facets of the same puzzle, and by doing so find your answer. It keeps you learning when the learning might stop. And continued life learning is a big part of The Difference.

When you engage in activities like word and number games, crossword puzzles, brainteasers, and Sudoku, your nerve cells can grow new connections, which research says makes you sharper over time. Why? They send a steady flow of oxygen to your brain, which essentially works to make you smarter. Even better, they can also help ward off Alzheimer's and dementia.

And, according to our study, a flexible brain can make you richer and more successful. Look at our movers who jumped from the bottom two groups to the top two. Although, as I noted in chapter 1, an overdose of creativity can hurt (the sort that makes it untenable for you to perform the sometimes monotonous tasks that are required to get ahead in work and in life), creativity in moderation is a very good thing.

Attribute	Describes Me	Percent More Likely to Move Forward Than Those Who Said the Word Didn't Describe Them at All
Creative	Slightly	14 percent
	Well	17 percent
	Very well	16 percent
	Completely	12 percent

So how do you encourage your creative genius if you don't have the flexible-thinking thing down pat? Isen's research shows that it helps to be in a good mood. (This is one of those times I told you about where the research starts crisscrossing. Optimism and happiness boost the ability to learn. Continued learning, in turn, boosts wealth—as well as your mood. Exercise alleviates stress, which boosts your mood, which boosts learning, which boosts . . . well, you get the idea.)

When you feel good, you naturally think more flexibly. It's not a matter of learning to do it or even trying to do it; just a mild warm feeling of optimism in your day can encourage you to turn the puzzle around and try to solve it from the other side. Why does this happen? Research is still ongoing, but Isen explains that when a positive event occurs, dopamine is released. It activates the frontal region of the brain, which enables you to not only think more, but think more flexibly.

Exercise: Improve Your Mood, Improve Your Flexible Thinking

You'd be surprised how little is required to boost your mood. It's not a matter of winning the lottery or popping a Prozac. In a recent study, Isen looked at the influence of a positive mood change induced by nothing major—a smile from a coworker, a small gift of ten wrapped hard candies in a sandwich bag, seeing five minutes of a funny movie—and found that these small things lead people to be more flexible in their thinking.

After bringing on a positive mood change, she tested flexible thinking and problem-solving ability two ways. She handed respondents a candle, matches, and a box of tacks and asked them to affix the candle to the wall in such a way that it didn't drip on the wall, the table, or the floor beneath it. (Could you do it? The answer is at the end of the chapter.) She then gave respondents three words and asked them to come up with a fourth word that links them together. Example: Mower. Atomic. Foreign. (Again, the answer is at the end of the chapter.) In both cases, the people in a good mood—who had seen the movie or received the smile or the candy—performed much better than those who were not.

How do you use this in your own life? For a week or so, take a few minutes each day to note three good things about your day. You should start to see a pattern—the same things emerging more than once. Make it a point to make time for those things on a more regular basis, even every day.

Answer to the candle problem: Dump the tacks out of the box and affix the box to the wall with a couple of tacks. Use the box as a candle holder to catch the dripping wax.

Answer to the word problem: Power.

A Quick Guide to Chapter 4

My college pal Susan—who went through a stretch where she didn't like her job much—had a saying: "That's why they have to pay you," she'd point out repeatedly. "If it was fun, you'd do it for free." I'd nod in agreement. We all have bad days. Some of us have bad months or even bad years.

After immersing myself in this research, however, I think we were both wrong. They—the employer, the client, the customer—have to pay you because what you're doing is valuable. But that doesn't mean it shouldn't be fun. Or stimulating. Or energizing. Or satisfying. The more passionate you are about your work, the more likely you are to find something you love and stick with it, and the more likely you are to get wealthy doing it. In this chapter, you'll figure out how to find your passion (or, in the interim, how to get a little more hot and bothered about what you're doing now) and how to translate it into financial success.

MEET SARA

AGE: Thirty-seven
ASSETS: 10 million–plus
FAMILY: Married
SARA'S DIFFERENCES: Takes risks, optimistic, flexible, connected

When Sara was in high school, she had a dream where she saw herself on the set of The Oprah Winfrey Show *chatting away with Oprah herself. So she did what any teenage girl would do. She blabbed to her friends. "It became this big running joke," she says as she laughs today. But a decade later, there she was, on the set. "It felt so right, so on-path," says Sara—Sara Blakely, the inventor of Spanx. "I was a little surprised that I was talking to her about footless panty hose, though. I never could have guessed that."*

Q: How did you get started?

A: I had these white pants that had been hanging in my closet for eight months, and I hadn't worn them because I just didn't like how my butt looked in them. One day I pulled them out, cut the feet off some panty hose, and put them on underneath. And it worked, except the panty hose kept riding up my legs. I thought, "I need to figure out how to make this stay comfortably just below the knee, because the material is thin and comfortable, and it can make you look three to five pounds thinner."

Q: So many people have what they think are "brilliant" ideas. Most just get talked about at cocktail parties and abandoned. What makes you different?

A: Well, it wasn't money. I didn't have a lot of money. I had $5,000 in savings, and that is to this day the only money I put into Spanx. I've been self-funded from the very start. I just knew from my own experience, you are your own focus group. So when I saw that this homemade solution worked better than anything else I could find or buy, I knew I was on to something.

And I started trying to find anyone who could help me make it. I went to every fabric store in town, and I went on the Internet and looked up hosiery mills and started calling them. No one would give me the time of day.

Q: Why didn't you give up?

A: At that point, I was selling fax machines door to door. So I was used to hearing no. That laid the groundwork for me to have the gumption to do my own thing—when you do, you're going to hear no.

It got worse. I decided to patent my invention. So I went to three law firms in Atlanta and presented my idea, and the lawyers were all laughing, too. One lawyer later admitted to me he thought my idea was so bad, he thought I'd been sent by *Candid Camera*. They were all men. I don't think there was a female patent attorney in the state of Georgia at that time.

So I bought a book on patents and trademarks and wrote my own patent. Then I took a week off of work and drove around North Carolina begging mill owners to make the footless concept. I kept thinking, "Where are the women?" That was why panty hose were so uncomfortable for so long. These male mill owners just didn't get it.

Q: During that week, did you have your breakthrough?
A: No. But I just had to do this. I didn't have a choice. I would cry, drive around the block and listen to motivational tapes, and try to convince myself to try again. I'm very big into visualization. I saw myself as the successful owner of Spanx. I was walking door-to-door, getting escorted out of buildings, but I knew my life would be different. I kept visualizing success.

Q: Eventually, you had a breakthrough, right?
A: It was about two or three weeks after I did the rounds of North Carolina that I got a phone call from a mill owner I'd seen. He said, "Sara, I've decided to help you make your crazy idea."

Q: He had daughters, didn't he?
A: Two.

Q: I knew it.
A: *I willed it.* It was an absolute belief that this would happen to me. I believe you can take mental snapshots of your future and what success looks like to you. If you mentally see yourself in a scenario, you'll start to make decisions in your life that get you there. I was very specific in what I wanted; I was exploring what I was good at, what my talents were. I knew I could sell and I didn't want to spend all day selling fax machines for someone else and making little money doing it.

The minute I cut the feet out of panty hose, I didn't question it. I knew it was what I'd been looking for. A lot of women come up to me and say, "Why didn't I think of that?" I think the difference is that I knew that I was looking for a business, I just hadn't figured out what that business would be.

Q: What do you tell other people who are looking for their business, their calling?

A: You have to come across an idea that you really want or that fills a need in the marketplace, or come up with an idea that significantly improves on something that already exists. One notch better and you're off and running. I took an existing product and cut the feet out of it to make a multimillion-dollar business.

You also have to be really focused. A lot of people get caught up in patenting and not wanting to discuss their idea in fear that they're going to get knocked off. If someone is going to knock you off, it's going to happen after they see the product in the marketplace, and at that point you were already the first out there.

And name it something really clever or different. If you can make someone laugh with your product's name, you're going to get an extra thirty seconds with them. I wrote down names for a year, and I narrowed down my thinking. I started thinking about Coca-Cola and Kodak, and what those names had in common. It's a weird trade secret among comedians that the "K" sound will make your audience laugh. The word "Spanks" came to me in traffic in Atlanta, and then at the last minute I changed the "ks" to an "X" because I knew it was easier to trademark made-up words.

Q: Once you had your product, how did you make it such a success?

A: I often say ignorance can be your greatest asset. I'd never done this before, I didn't know how this was done. If no one showed you how to do your job, how would you do it? You're never going to create change or invent something if you're just doing it the way it's always been done. So I just picked up the phone and called the hosiery buyer from Neiman Marcus. When cold calling you don't leave messages, so I called for five days before she picked up the phone. I told her that I had invented a product that her customers wouldn't be able to live without, and that it would make a big difference in the store's clothing. I told her I'd fly there if she gave me ten minutes, and she said fine.

I jumped on a plane and met with her, and five minutes into my pitch, I told her she needed to come with me into the bathroom. I showed her my white pants with and without Spanx and she said, "It's brilliant! I want it in seven stores as a trial." Then I called everyone I knew in those seven cities and asked them to please buy my product. There was no way I wasn't going to let those fly off the shelves, even if I had to take out my own loan and buy all of the products myself.

CHAPTER FOUR

Ding, Dong, Your Passion Is Calling

Follow your bliss. Find your passion. Do what you love.

We have, every single one of us, heard those words. And we are clearly trying. At least if trying is something you can measure in hours on the clock. Data from the 2008 study of the National Sleep Foundation shows the average worker spends nine and a half hours at the workplace each day topped off by another four and a half hours working from home. That's a fourteen-hour workday.

But the psychic benefit of all this work clearly isn't registering. About a million people a day phone in sick. In this country we spend about $150 billion per year in treatment for stress-related problems, absenteeism, reduced productivity, and employee turnover, according to Jane Boucher's *How to Love the Job You Hate: Job Satisfaction for the 21st Century.* And research from the Conference Board shows that only 50 percent of people are satisfied with their jobs today. That's down from 79 percent in 1985, which represents a huge slide in the past twenty years.

On the other hand, the wealthy, and to some degree the financially comfortable, tell a different story. They are far more likely to like what they do, and significantly more likely to say they are "passionate" about it.

"I am passionate about my work."

	Percent That Agreed
Wealthy	44 percent
Financially comfortable	39 percent
Paycheck-to-paychecks	33 percent
Further-in-Debtors	33 percent

Perhaps this is because they've always had some sense of what line of work would fit them best. They were far less likely to switch from major to major in college until they ended up on the five- or six-year plan struggling to find the right path.

"I have always known what I wanted to do for a career."

	Percent That Agreed
Wealthy	32 percent
Financially comfortable	22 percent
Paycheck-to-paychecks	16 percent
Further-in-debtors	14 percent

And perhaps thanks to this knowledge, the wealthy are far less likely to have swapped in and out of careers.

This is a striking finding. Today, it's expected that Americans will—over a life of work—have around twelve different jobs in four different fields. Those are the averages. Some people have more. The wealthy and financially comfortable have fewer.

How many times, on average, have you changed your occupation in your adult life?

	Percent That Agreed
Wealthy	2.1
Financially comfortable	2.8
Paycheck-to-paychecks	3.5
Further-in-debtors	4

Why? Duke's David Robinson notes that some of the wealthy have graduate degrees—JDs or MDs—that set them up for one occupation that they're likely to stick with (at least while they pay off all their student debt). As you'll see on the chart below, a greater percentage of the wealthy identify themselves as professionals such as doctors and lawyers than as managers or business owners.

Over the course of your career, how would you describe your various occupations?

	Business Owner	Technical	Professional	Managerial
Wealthy	21 percent	25 percent	44 percent	43 percent
Financially comfortable	13 percent	23 percent	33 percent	38 percent
Paycheck-to-paychecks	12 percent	15 percent	22 percent	29 percent
Further-in-debtors	11 percent	13 percent	18 percent	28 percent

But the wealthy and financially comfortable also isolated their passions early on. They have—in their own words—"always" had some sense of what sort of work or career they wanted to pursue. So staying on course doesn't represent the sort of challenge it does for people who feel unsure or are wavering.

There are benefits to consistency. When we in the press talk about job movement, we usually do it in positive terms. Moving from one company to the next is often the best way to increase your compensation. But there's a downside. According to Hewitt Associates, about half of all workers drain their retirement accounts when they move from one job to another. And they pay up to 40 percent of the balance to Uncle Sam in the form of taxes and penalties, rather than rolling those funds into a new 401(k) or an IRA where the tax benefits are preserved and the money can continue to grow. Smaller balances tend to be cashed out more often, so if an individual changes jobs several times and cashes out, every time they'll potentially end up with nothing. If they don't cash out but continue to change jobs before they're fully vested—44 percent of companies vest their employees immediately, but the rest don't—they'll still lose out. You risk losing employer contributions, which are a significant part of retirement savings.

Moreover, when a job change involves a career change, you may need to take a step back in terms of the corporate hierarchy, which can translate into lower pay, less seniority, and perhaps never reaching your full earning potential.

Two Ways to Solve the Problem

Here's what we know: People who are passionate about what they do reach financial comfort and wealth more often than those who are not. That means you should (a) find your passion and pursue it, or (b) get passionate about what you're already doing. Let's start with the former.

The First Option: Do What You Love

A few months after I started my job at *Working Woman* magazine, a new editorial assistant named Laurel Touby was hired to sit at the next desk. She was different from the rest of us. A little louder. A little more eccentric. We used to call her the "portable party." In fact, that was what she loved to do in her spare time—throw parties.

After *Working Woman,* she moved to *BusinessWeek.* While she was there, Laurel started throwing networking parties for people in the media. She would host each event (always wearing a red feather boa, so that people could pick her out of the crowd) and invite people to one bar or another to buy their own drinks and talk about ways they could help one another get ahead in their careers.

She called this enterprise Media Bistro. The parties became immensely popular, and she found that she was the owner of a huge list of e-mail addresses for people in the media. Eventually that list became a website featuring the media news of the day, and a revolving list of who's been fired and who's been hired. A few years later, someone suggested to her that she start offering Learning Annex–style classes, to teach the mediabistro.com population how to write screenplays, do service journalism, and transition from print into broadcast. So she did that, too. And in 2007 she sold this little party business to Jupiter Media for $23 million. All because she was able to focus in on her passion, understand what it was telling her, and blow it out of the water.

How do you do the same?

You start by identifying those things that "might" be on your list and those things that most definitely are not. Asking yourself these questions can help you figure that out. Try to be as honest as possible with your answers. You're not roped into changing your life based on what you say or feel here, but unless you allow yourself to go deep, you're missing the point.

TEN QUESTIONS TO PINPOINT YOUR PASSIONS

1. If money was *not* an issue, what would you be doing with your life?

2. When you go to the magazine racks or the library, what do you most like to read about? (Alternately, what do you find yourself searching for on the Internet?)

3. Think about the last few times you said to yourself: "I'd like to do that sometime." What was "that"?

4. What do other people say you do particularly well?

5. Think back to when you were ten or twelve and try to remember how it felt to be really excited about the possibility of doing something. What could you do today that might make you feel the same way?

6. What do you secretly dream about doing?

7. What are the things you like about what you're doing now? (They can be small, but you have to name several of them.)

8. What do you think you do particularly well? (These things do not have to be work related.)

9. How do you feel you contribute or could contribute to society?

10. What do you want your children or friends to say about you when you're gone?

As you answer the questions, you'll see patterns emerge. They may reflect hidden desires: things that you've perhaps buried or that you wanted in the past but haven't thought about for a while. Or they may reflect desires you know full well you have, but have not—for financial to emotional reasons—pursued.

If you're going to move toward these desires, they have to come out. In this way, passions are like other goals. If you haven't articulated them and broken down the steps that need to be taken to reach them, they're very difficult to attain. Once you've got a grip on what they are, you need to understand how you can make them happen.

Can You Do It a Little Bit Better?

"Tweaking" has been one of my favorite words since I heard Tom Hanks use it in *You've Got Mail* to describe the process he was going through to woo an unsuspecting Meg Ryan. It means making something better, improving it—not a great deal, just . . . enough.

Sara Blakely was not the first person to take scissors to panty hose. Two decades ago, I was cutting the control top off pairs of L'eggs because I found they worked better than most strapless bras. What I didn't do was consider my idea brilliant and take it to market. I didn't pick up the phone and call the buyer at Neiman Marcus and later drag her to the bathroom to try on my newfangled brassiere. Sara Blakely tweaked an idea that I am sure others had before she did. And now she is a very wealthy, very successful woman.

There are three types of vision. There are people who can see something completely new. Think of Henry Ford and cars for the masses. There are those who take something that's been done before and make it better or put it to a different use. Think of Sam Walton. He didn't invent retailing. He didn't even invent discounting. But he did it better than it had been done before. And then there are people who figure out what they're good at and do it over and over again. Think of Kathie Lee Gifford, who is having a resurgence (and getting great reviews) on the new fourth hour of the *Today* show. She's great at morning television. Why not fill a need, improve the ratings, and pad her own wallet as a result?

The point is, you have to bring something to the party that isn't at the party already. It can be your product. It can be your tenacity or your energy. It can be the length you are willing to go to make your endeavor a success.

Getting out of your dream or vision and into real life means being action oriented. You may set your sights on the heavens, but you need to be grounded in reality.

Can You Make It Profitable?

Here's an unfortunate fact of modern life: It's not enough to be good at something. You can be the best baker, the best shopkeeper, the best designer. The world is littered with bests. You need to be able to take that attribute and put it into a framework that works. Doug Harrison, a noted market researcher, told me a story of a conversation he had with a couple who makes what they described as "the best" cheese and yogurt butter. They asked him what he thought about starting their own business. And he said, "Think about it in business terms. To get started, you'll need a minimum of $150,000 in gross revenue. How many units do you need to sell per day to reach that? How many units per hour? How does that fit in with your current distribution?"

"These questions weren't even on their radar," he says. "The mistake people make is stopping their thinking at the point of 'I make the best cheese and yogurt butter.' Those thoughts aren't complete. They're not sufficient to get where they need to be."

Sara Blakely wouldn't have succeeded with Spanx had she not found a manufacturer and placed the products in stores. Doug Harrison's experience with his own marketing research firm was similar. Early in his business he had a set of clients signed up for services. But the business was vulnerable. If any of those clients had decided to go elsewhere for research, it would have been hard to pay the employees, much less the rent. So he scaled up, adding a big sales and marketing department to increase the number of clients so that no one loss could rock the boat. "Before it was like having a hobby, rather than having a business," he says.

Don't Quit Your Day Job

One thing to consider: Are your finances nimble enough to accommodate this sort of shift? It's an important question. You may be driven to let your passion consume your work life, but if you are unable to make ends meet while you're in transition, the entire process has the potential to be very stressful. Here are a few suggestions for smoothing the ride.

TAKE A TEST DRIVE. Pretend you're living on a reduced income for several months. See if you can actually swing it. This is what I advise couples who are expecting a child and want to see if they can afford for one parent to stay home. Figure out how much your cash flow will be compromised, and see if you can make ends meet. The longer you can sustain the experiment the better it is for your bottom line. Why?

Banking the difference between your current real income and your future "pretend" one will beef up your emergency stash.

TRIM YOUR DEBTS. You won't take much psychic pleasure in your new life if your old mortgage payment is stressing you out every month. So consider downsizing. Keep your old, paid-off car rather than saddling yourself with a new monthly payment. And keep the credit cards at arm's length.

WEIGH THE FINANCIAL VARIABLES. There are more of these than you may think. Will you need extra schooling and training? Will you suffer a possible decline in Social Security benefits because you'll be earning less for a few years? Who will pay for your health care or match contributions to your retirement account? Will you continue to live where you are, or move somewhere where taxes and living costs are higher or lower?

HOW LONG WILL IT BE BEFORE YOU'RE IN THE BLACK? If you expect you will be in belt-tightening mode for a bit, how long will that period last? Knowing this is key to keeping your spending in check for as long as you'll need to. Having as much information as possible will help you not only hit the ground running, but ensure you are able to sustain that pace.

The Second Option: Love What You Do

There is, of course, a downside to finding your passion and then transitioning to pursue it. It takes time. Perhaps considerable time. So here's an alternative—and it's one to consider even if you are aiming to make that bigger transition in the long term: Learn to love what you do. Yes. It's possible.

There are jobs. There are careers. And then there are callings. Amy Wrzesniewski of Yale University School of Management is the top researcher in this area, and she explains: A job is something you do every day for a paycheck. It is a means to an end, but you are not personally invested. A career is a paycheck with the ability to advance. And a calling is something you simply have to do. You'd do it even if you didn't get paid. What Wrzesniewski and others who've studied these differences have learned is that these labels don't attach themselves to particular jobs. They attach themselves to how you feel about your work. There are doctors and lawyers for whom work is a job; others for whom it is a career; and others for whom it is a calling. Likewise, there are hospital custodians for whom work is a job; others for whom it is a career; and others for whom it is a calling.

Really. Wrzesniewski studied them to see if even people in what many would consider the most menial jobs would see a way to rise above. Some did. Wrzesniewski found that when asked to describe their work, those who saw it as a job would say: "I clean eighteen rooms," while those who saw it as a calling would say: "I take care of the pediatrics unit." Cleaners who saw their work as a calling would talk about the work that they do taking care of patients, or how it was part of the healing process. They did their jobs with care, pride, and consistency, missed fewer days of work, and had better performance reviews. Their incomes—over time—reflected that difference.

Why is it that some hospital cleaners—just like some doctors and lawyers—see the value in what they're doing and others see drudgery? The study took into account many variables: high-traffic units, low-traffic units, males versus females, race, tenure, night shift versus day shift. None of those things made a significant difference. Wrzesniewski believes the difference in perception is partly due to a person's disposition and partly to a person's general idea of what work is and what it's supposed to mean. Just like happiness, resilience, and many of the other attributes we'll discuss in later chapters, it's something you can change. If you want to find more of the good in the work you're doing—more of the value—and make it more of a calling, you can do just that. The question is: How?

Find the Calling in Your Job or Career

FORGE A PERSONAL CONNECTION WITH YOUR BOSS. If you're working for someone you feel is charismatic or inspirational, you're likely to want to perform better in that person's eyes. You can't take an uncharismatic supervisor and turn him or her into Gandhi, of course. But perhaps you haven't gotten to know the person who is managing you—and that person may have leadership characteristics that you haven't noticed. Schedule a breakfast meeting. (Yes, breakfast. Those early morning hours signal your willingness to jump in off the clock. Lunch can simply be an indicator that you're looking to kick back in the middle of the day.)

FIND AUTONOMY IN YOUR JOB. The cleaners who felt a calling went above and beyond their job descriptions. They interacted with patients. They asked how they were feeling. They refilled water glasses. Nobody told them to do these things. But nobody told them not to, either. Autonomy is key to feeling good about the work you do, no matter what kind of work it is. Research has shown you'll be happier at work if you can make your own mark—whether you do it by moving the couch in your office from one side of the room to the other, or by scheduling your meetings at 11 a.m. while everyone else holds theirs at 4 p.m. In other words, striking out for independence doesn't have to be a battle cry, it can be a whisper and have the same mood-elevating results.

DON'T STOP TO SMELL THE ROSES—DO NOTICE THEM. Small positive things happen every day. You're not necessarily directly involved in them, they may just be around you. They may not even be human. Good weather, a nice painting on the wall, the fact that today's office coffee is better than the usual sludge: All are small positive things. Don't ignore them. Don't push them out of your mind. Take a second to acknowledge what's good around you. Many people believe that happiness at work is a new six-figure account. Research shows that's not the case. These small positives make a significant difference, but only if you register them.

FAKE IT TILL YOU MAKE IT, PART 1. Have you ever heard anyone say something like, "I'm so absentminded. I always misplace my keys." After a while, it becomes a self-fulfilling prophecy. Unless one day that key loser decides to put a hook on the wall and hang the keys there the minute he walks in the door. All of a sudden, he isn't so absentminded anymore. While you're trying to find the satisfaction in your work, pretend you already feel satisfied. Tell yourself you had a good day. Walk through the corridors with a smile rather than a scowl on your face. Here's what will happen: Your positive energy will radiate. The person in the next office won't be scared you'll jump down her throat if she asks you if you caught last night's *30 Rock,* so she might just start a conversation. Your boss might think you're interviewing. Either way, all of a sudden your work looks more intriguing. If you act like you're having fun, you will have fun. I'm not promising you a party. But I can guarantee an improvement.

CHANGE JOBS, NOT CAREERS. If you've tried all of the above and you're still not able to find some on-the-job satisfaction, the problem may be with the organization, not with you. Yale University School of Management's Amy Wrzesniewski looked at a group of registered nurses who went into their work thinking they would find great meaning in it but instead found just the opposite. What happened? The organization drained them of their passion. Every day, they found themselves running around like mad on their shifts, trying to stop one disaster or another. Notes Wrzesniewski, "It becomes unsustainable to have meaning in the work if the organization isn't allowing you to experience it that way." Time to start interviewing. This time, look for a boss who inspires you, colleagues who seem pleased to be there, and a culture that values the independent ideas and talents you'd bring to the place.

When You Get Close, Stop Looking

As I have said, having choices is good. Autonomy is essential. But too many choices can get in the way of happiness—and being unhappy (as you'll see in the next chapter) can impede your success. Swarthmore College professor Barry Schwartz, author of *The Paradox of Choice: Why Less Is More,* studied college seniors from fifteen different academic institutions as they interviewed for jobs. When they started the process, he asked them to classify what they were looking for. Some said "the best job." Others said "a job." What happened? The students who were looking for the best jobs found jobs that paid on average 20 percent more. But they were not satisfied. The students who were looking for any job were paid on average 20 perent less. But they were happier.

By standard measures of success, pushing, pushing, and then pushing some more may get you there. But if what you want is success *and* a good feeling about whatever you've been able to achieve—in other words, some modicum of balance—you need to think positively about what you have and appreciate it, before you reach for more.

You may think that you don't know how to do this. That it's impossible to slow down or take a smaller step. But, Schwartz points out, everybody does this in some parts of their lives. You may go to the grocery store looking for Kellogg's Raisin Bran and find only Post, or vice versa. Or Skippy peanut butter when you wanted Jif. Do you tell yourself it's "good enough" and eat it just the same? Can you apply this same sensibility to your work life? The more areas of your life in which you can feel this way, the research shows, the happier you'll be. Notes Schwartz: This is true of important things as well as trivial ones. You can tell yourself you want the best job, romantic partner, and medical care—and that you'll settle on other things—but that's a recipe for misery. (It's also a recipe for romantic relationships that last about a minute.) But if you can find the willingness to endure short-term frustrations, to compartmentalize the parts of your work that are not enjoyable and put them in a place where they won't impede your ability to get the good out of the other parts, the overall payoff can be huge.

Exercise: Visualize the Next Logical Step

Whether you're taking the first approach or the second—finding the work you love or learning to love the work you do—it will help if you can visualize what comes next. As I noted earlier in the chapter, the vast majority of people who are visionary do not invent the next great operating system. They take what's already there and move it one logical step further. So every day for the next week, take fifteen minutes out of your day to consider what you want next. It should be a fifteen-minute period when your brain is at its best. Grab your legal pad or sit down at your computer and imagine what's possible. Once you have your short list, rate your ideas on a scale of 1 to 10 on these two criteria:

1. Can you own this idea? Is this something you could implement—on a small scale or a big one—get credit for it, and feel good about it?

2. Can you prosper from it? No, it's not all about the money. But money is a barometer of success and achievement. And if this next logical step will bring some your way, it's another way for you to feel rewarded.

Exercise: Build a Passion

Sure, some people are born knowing they have to be doctors or landscape artists or architects. Others are not, but you can—if you have a sliver of interest in something—turn it into a passion. How? By learning more about it, then practicing it (if, like cooking or karate, it is something that can be practiced). Doing something that scares you or makes you nervous is actually a signal that you may be on the right track. If not knowing how to do something has you feeling like an idiot, it's an indication that you care about doing it better.

A Quick Guide to Chapter 5

Some people believe that money leads to happiness. It's an ongoing argument, and the latest research seems to indicate there's a threshold: Money leads to happiness only up to a point—how much is relative, national, and regional. But after that point, the next Mercedes in the driveway isn't going to make much of a difference.

Reverse this, however, and you've a much stronger case. Happiness—without a doubt—leads to money and success. So does optimism. Both enable you to solve problems, conjure ideas, take long-range consequences into consideration, and come back and try again if you miss the first time.

You don't want to be overly happy or overly optimistic, though— that can lead to a loss of competitive juices that are helpful in making The Difference a part of your life. In this chapter, you'll learn what separates happiness from optimism, how to use new research to attain the right amounts of each, and how—perhaps more than any of the other attributes we'll discuss in this book—happiness and optimism have direct links to all the others. They make the most difference.

MEET JANE

AGE: Sixty-nine
FAMILY: Married, two children
ASSETS: $1.5 million to $2.5 million
JANE'S DIFFERENCES: Financially comfortable, grateful, optimistic, always learning, always saving

Many of the people profiled in this book are optimists. It's one of the attributes that showed up in the research more than most others. So why is Jane's interview here, instead of one of the many others? Because toward the end of a delightful interview—during which she made us smile with her memories of shopping at Sears and a plea to women to get their own checkbooks (please!)—she revealed that the very next day she'd be undergoing major surgery for cancer. The fact that she was still looking toward tomorrow in such an upbeat way tipped the scales in her favor.

Q: We've found that a fair number of our financially comfortable people were either teachers or had parents who were teachers.

A: It's funny that you mention that, because both my husband and I worked for an educational nonprofit. Both my husband and I were in a defined-contribution plan. You put money in and it grows for you tax-deferred. We started out with not very much money. We lived comfortably, but we always saved, and so we were able to retire at fifty-nine and a half.

Q: What percentage of your income did you save?

A: In the beginning, not that much. If you saved 3 percent, the company would match it. It was a no-brainer. Then, after my girls graduated from college, both my husband and I put away the maximum amount allowed by law. It wasn't reflected as a percentage, it was $9,500 fixed. Since then, the amount has gone up.

Q: Did you control the asset allocation?

A: Some of it was controlled by TIAA-CREF. The company also allowed employees to put money into other companies' mutual funds, and I did allocate some of the money into Fidelity Magellan and Vanguard Windsor, both excellent funds. At the time, Peter Lynch was running Fidelity Magellan, and John Bogle was running Vanguard Windsor.

Q: You can't ask for more than that. Both those guys are statesmen of the industry. Did you always work?

A: I was a stay-at-home mom for the first years of our marriage. I went to work in 1975 and retired in June 1997. That was twenty-two years with the same company.

Q: Did you ever feel tempted to pull your money out of the mutual funds, say when the stock market crashed in 1987?

A: No, I just kept putting money in. My philosophy was that the stock market was relative—that if I lost a lot of money, so did everybody else. And when the stock market went up, everybody made a lot of money, but I wouldn't make as much as some of the big players.

Q: Aah, so you're an optimist. I also see you identify yourself as "grateful." What are you grateful about?

A: I'm not sure that "grateful" is the right word. "Glad" is a better description of the way I feel. I am glad that I was able to accomplish this. I don't credit anybody else, except maybe my husband. This was something we decided to do together.

Q: What motivated the two of you to keep saving all those years? Maybe you wanted to live in a house on the water when you retired, or you wanted to be able to travel?

A: I have to laugh. We just moved to a town house that backs up to a pond, so I do have a house on the water. And we do travel. But our goals were a little more mundane: We both wanted to get to a point where we didn't have to worry about money.

Q: What was there to be worried about?

A: My mother was never quite happy. She never thought she had enough money. My parents lived through the Depression. In my household when I was growing up, we had barely enough, but it was adequate. I can remember vividly the day my parents paid off the house and they had a mortgage-burning party.

When we were first married, we had enough to live on and not much more than that. Still, we managed to do a lot of things with our children. We went camping. We didn't spend a lot of money going to expensive resorts. My husband and I both felt that we wanted to save because we didn't want to be in a lot of debt. Back in those days, you bought everything from Sears. If you needed a new washer, you went to Sears. If you needed tires for the car, you went to Sears. We didn't have other credit cards, but we had a revolving charge with Sears. At first, besides saving money for the girls' college, our goal was to get to a point where we didn't owe Sears money.

And still, it wasn't until I went back to work to put the kids through college (they were ten and fifteen when I went back) that we had more money. We had promised the children that we would pay for four years of college, regardless. For graduate school they were on their own, but both of our daughters worked for companies that paid for them to go to graduate school.

Q: Was it easy for you to jump back into the workforce after being away for fifteen years?

A: I was a secretary before I was married. I went back as a secretary. I slowly worked my way up from secretary to more and more responsible positions in the company. I worked for a company where that was possible.

Q: Did they send you for training?

A: Not really. Whatever I learned, I learned on my own. I had a range of jobs. Spent the bulk of my career in human resources. I retired as the director of employee benefits, and most of what I learned, I learned on the job. At first, I said, "I'll only work till the kids are through college." But I liked working. So I continued to work until I had been there twenty years so I could qualify for the retirement plan that gave you medical benefits. That's nice to have. I've been enjoying life ever since I retired.

Q: You sound much happier than your own mother. Have you passed that optimism on to your daughters?

A: I try not to tell my daughters what to do. By example, they know what we have done. But I have two extremely different daughters. One is married to a man who is a saver. My other daughter likes to spend and she married someone who likes to spend. I spend my time keeping my mouth shut.

But I do tell them one thing. The most common mistake I've seeen is that women cede total control of their money to their husbands, even if they are working. One of the things I did was serve on my company's credit union board. We would meet and decide whether to lend money to people. Between that and being in the benefits department, I saw a lot of women who had no credit in their own name, who didn't handle their own money. Even when they applied for a loan or a mortgage from the credit union, they brought their husbands in to fill out the form and answer questions. When their husbands died, they had no idea what to do. So the message I wanted to get to them, and my daughters—and every woman—was please get your own checkbook! At least find out where the bank is that is holding the family money. There were so many women who didn't know that it was disturbing.

CHAPTER FIVE

Get Happy
(But Not Too Happy)

Checked out the *New York Times* bestseller list in recent years? In February 2008, you might have spotted multiple appearances by Marci Shimoff's *Happy for No Reason: Seven Steps for Being Happy from the Inside Out*. The following month, *The Geography of Bliss: One Grump's Search for the Happiest Places in the World* by former NPR foreign correspondent Eric Weiner hit it big. Both of these followed on the heels of *Stumbling on Happiness* by Harvard psychologist Daniel Gilbert, which spent umpteen weeks on that list and others, eventually being translated into twenty languages.

Clearly, happiness is something we feel is worth striving for. And with good reason. There are many other worthwhile things that go along with being happy. Happy people are healthier. They live longer because they do things like apply sunscreen regularly and stick with a doctor's prescribed regimen, even years after a medical event—such as a bypass—that could have done them in. Happy people are more likely to achieve their goals because, the research tells us, it's easier to make progress toward those goals when you're in a good frame of mind.

And—for a whole litany of reasons—happy people are more suc-cessful. They are more likely to graduate from college, to land job interviews, and to get those jobs. On the job, they receive better perfor-mance evaluations, not just from their bosses but from their colleagues. Happy people tend to be more productive, more creative, more de-pendable, and produce higher quality work. They get promoted and their salaries rise accordingly.

In other words, although wealth cannot buy you happiness, happi-ness does seem to be able to "buy" you money. The connection is ap-parent when you look back at our research.

Are you happy?	
	Yes
Wealthy	55 percent
Financially comfortable	56 percent
Paycheck-to-paychecks	39 percent
Further-in-debtors	32 percent

But the trajectory becomes clearer when you look specifically at our movers, those who were further in debt or lived paycheck to pay-check and are now financially comfortable or wealthy.

Attribute	Describes Me	Percent More Likely to Move Forward Than Those Who Said the Word Didn't Describe Them at All
Happy	Slightly	14 percent
	Well	21 percent
	Very well	29 percent
	Completely	19 percent

Testing our movers' optimism had similar results.

Attribute	Describes Me	Percent More Likely to Move Forward Than Those Who Said the Word Didn't Describe Them at All
Optimism	Slightly	16 percent
	Well	29 percent
	Very well	27 percent
	Completely	29 percent

And it's not just true in this country or this study. A 2005 study of Malaysian farmers found that happiness predicted material wealth, as did a 2004 study of twenty-four thousand people in Germany. And two Russian studies, the first in 1995 and the second in 2000, revealed a strong correlation between happiness and wealth.

The Happiness-Wealth Connection

Before moving on, I want to spend just a little time on the money and happiness connection. About one-third of people believe that money can buy you happiness. They're right. And they're wrong.

In the United States at least, money buys you happiness—only up to a point. If it's lifting you out of poverty, enabling you to pay your rent or put food on the table or take a sick child to the pediatrician, having that additional cash drastically improves your quality of life and therefore makes you happier. But once you're comfortable, more money doesn't buy you more happiness. In the United States people have gotten richer and richer in the post–World War II decades and yet there's been no bump in national happiness.

On the world stage, more money seems to make a greater difference than it does here at home. Richer countries are happier than moderately rich ones. The Gallup World Poll surveys citizens in 140 countries. It asked, "How satisfied are you with your life?" In richer countries, such as the United States, Japan, parts of Europe (particularly Scandinavia), and Saudi Arabia, most people say they are happy. In poor parts of the world—like many places in Africa—most people are not. Bottom line: When you have nothing or very little, some extra cash will put a smile on your face. Otherwise, you'll have to find that happiness elsewhere.

Happiness and Optimism Are Not the Same Thing

Interestingly, happiness and optimism are not synonymous. Happiness is what you're feeling today about how things are going in the short and long term. Academics refer to it as your sense of well-being. Optimism is a way of looking at the future. It's a tendency to believe you'll experience good rather than bad outcomes in life—that good things are going to be plentiful.

In short, happiness is about today. Optimism is about tomorrow. That's why the happiest countries are not necessarily the most optimistic. European countries, including France—where people are living well right now—are often happy, but they're not optimistic. This is according to an Ipsos poll that ranked twenty countries by asking such questions as "Will your children be better off than you are?" Developing countries such as China and India—where people are not well off right now, but GDP growth is off the charts—are the opposite of France. They're optimistic, but they're not happy.

Interestingly, on a national level, optimism—and pessimism— seem to be driven much more by women than by men. Why? They're the ones most concerned about their children.

In chapter 1, I classified Americans by their financial situations. You'll recall 15 percent are going further and further into debt each month, 54 percent are living paycheck to paycheck, 30 percent are financially comfortable, and just 3 percent are wealthy. This, by the way, is a big improvement over how these same Americans were doing ten years earlier. But how do they think they will fare about ten years from now?

Even in the midst of a rocky economy 80 percent of further-into-debtors believe they will be doing better. And 50 percent of the paycheck-to-paychecks believe they will be financially comfortable. In fact, the vast majority of the total population believe they will be financially comfortable or wealthy. That's optimism at work.

Optimism seems to be a naturally occuring brain function. Two neuroscientists from New York City recently studied brain activity in fifteen healthy volunteers and found that our brains light up more when we think about positive events that might occur in the future than when we dwell on negative ones. We give those events more of our brain power. That turns out to be fabulous news, because when it comes to your finances, there is no better weapon in your arsenal than a decent dose of positive thinking.

Are you optimistic?

	Yes
Wealthy	56 percent
Financially comfortable	54 percent
Paycheck-to-paychecks	40 percent
Further-in-debtors	31 percent

When It Comes to Money, You Want to Be Both Optimistic and Happy

Like happy people, optimists do well financially. They also do well on the job. Optimists work more hours, and they expect to retire later in life, thus building up bigger retirement stashes. Optimists not only save more, but more of their wealth is in liquid assets. They also invest more than pessimists in individual stocks and they are more likely to pay their credit card bills promptly. And when optimists divorce they are more likely than pessimists to remarry, which is also good for building wealth.

HABITS THAT HELP: MARRIAGE
HABITS THAT HURT: DIVORCE

Here's one thing we know about optimists—it takes at least one of them to sustain a romantic union. Happy individuals are even more likely than optimists to get married and stay married. And being married is good for your finances.

Whether two can live as cheaply as one is a point that has been endlessly debated. My take is that it depends on the two—do they combine their purchasing power for the greater good by moving into the apartment that previously sufficed for one, or do they see it as an opportunity to scale up and buy the McMansion and that third car—just for the weekends?

Research says that, on average, being married and living a combined lifestyle adds to your wealth. A 2006 study published in the *Journal of Sociology* looked at more than nine thousand baby boomers, age forty-one to forty-nine. It showed that married individuals had nest eggs 93 percent larger than single or divorced folks. (Divorce is its own wealth negator.) Moreover, married couples saw annual increases in their wealth of 16 percent, double the increases of singles.

In part, that's the cost of living talking—the impact of economies of scale. It's also because people who are married—or in a committed partnership—have reasons beyond themselves—their own wants and their own needs—to produce. They are working for the betterment of their growing family, with common goals such as paying down debt, buying that first (or larger) home, paying for college educations, supporting charities they believe in, retiring comfortably, and eventually passing a chunk of wealth along to their heirs. Married or coupled folks also have, in their partners, built-in sanity checks on their spending. If one partner treads too close to the line, blowing the budget on clothing or technology, the other is there to rein him or her in.

It's interesting that when divorce was studied, assets started dwindling four years before a divorce was final. Perhaps spouses started living apart, which costs more. But I suspect another factor was at work: Those spouses who saw their marriage coming to an end no longer felt the need to strive to add to their own little unit.

But Not Too Optimistic or Happy

What you don't want to be—it turns out—is a sap.

From the halls of academia, we are now learning that too much happiness and optimism is not a good thing. This represents something of a turnaround. University of Illinois professor Ed Diener explains that over the years he and colleagues have proven that people who are happier tend to make more money. A few years ago, however, investing guru John Templeton wrote Diener a letter that got the professor scratching his head. "Is life satisfaction always great?" Templeton asked. "Maybe dissatisfaction is okay. Maybe a little bit of dissatisfaction is okay."

"I started wondering," Diener says, "do you have to be happier and happier? How happy is happy enough?" Thus, a new study was born. Diener and his colleagues used data from the World Values Survey, which measures happiness on a scale of 1 (least happy) to 10 (happiest), and found that 10s not only earned less money than the 8s and the 9s, they earned significantly less. The 8s and 9s were also more likely to be further along in their education and more active in the political process than the 10s.

What's so good about being mildly happy? Why is it better financially than being euphoric? Mildly happy people are strivers. They're more interested in making the sort of changes necessary to get ahead in life—including engaging in competition (not always a happy pursuit) when necessary, going out and getting a higher education, and making behavioral changes when their current behavior isn't working. The 10s, on the other hand, are too self-satisfied to adjust.

This even seems to be the case in the classroom. Diener's team looked at success in an academic environment, ranking happiness this time not by numbers but by groups: unhappy, slightly happy, moderately happy, happy, or very happy. Then they took a look at how the students were doing academically by grade point average, class attendance, and several other factors. Academic success went up as happiness increased. But it peaked at "happy" and fell back for "very happy." The happy group even outperformed the very happy group where grades were concerned.

Why does this happen? When you're blissful, you become complacent. As long as your approach (to work, life, love, whatever) is working, why would you try anything new? The downside is that when that approach stops working, you may not recognize it.

Think of the experience retailers go through every day. A store like the Gap can have such huge success selling khakis, it is inclined to keep trying to sell them—and to do so with yet another round of those dance-filled commercials that were originally so fresh. But as the Gap was doing the same thing that worked the last time, the mind-set of the shopper changed. We didn't want those pants anymore. We had seen enough of those commercials—we didn't even care if this time around they starred Sarah Jessica Parker.

The same thing can happen to an individual at work. As a writer, for example, at *SmartMoney* magazine in the early '90s, I went through a period where I did a number of what I came to think of as "kitchen sink" stories. Everything a smart consumer needs to know about insurance. Everything a smart consumer needs to know about divorce. They were met with enthusiasm when I pitched them in our monthly story idea meetings. Until one day, they weren't. The editors were tired of hearing these same things from me, and it was time to come up with something else. Feeling too self-satisfied is not great for your career. Why? Because you're inclined to fight upper management. You feel that righteousness a little too deeply. You're better off with a degree of self-doubt. It allows you to not only see another person's point of view but also come around to it from time to time.

Diener is not the only researcher on this quest. When Duke's David Robinson and his colleagues undertook an examination of optimists, they also found that people who saw the glass as too full (classified as people who overestimated their own life spans by twenty years or more) behaved in ways that were not good for their future. They overspent. They accumulated debt. They didn't save. Mild optimists save more, and their savings tend to be in liquid assets. They are more likely to have emergency funds, because they think there is a greater chance of emergencies.

"I believe I will have much more money in the future than I have now."

	Percent That Agreed
Wealthy	43 percent
Financially comfortable	25 percent
Paycheck-to-paychecks	21 percent
Further-in-debtors	23 percent

"I save regularly for the future."

	Percent That Agreed
Wealthy	60 percent
Financially comfortable	38 percent
Paycheck-to-paychecks	9 percent
Further-in-debtors	6 percent

Everything in Moderation

This need for moderation spills over into other parts of life, notes Robinson. When you compare moderate optimists to more extreme ones, one of the biggest areas of difference is self-control. Moderate optimists are less likely to be smokers (see box, page 230). Extreme optimists are more likely. Moderate optimists are more likely to take their vitamins; extreme optimists are not. Extreme optimists assume things are going to take care of themselves. Mild optimists can more clearly envision future difficulties and take action so that the future is better.

The emotional system, properly working, is your ally. You want your emotional defenses to register that there's a bear chasing you, so that you'll be afraid and run a little faster. But you don't want your fight-or-flight responses to shoot to the top with every little cricket on your tail. You want to spend your time and energy on potential problems, not small mistakes. Otherwise you'll never get anything done.

Fear, anger, sadness, anxiety, and other negative emotions are trouble when they're chronic but helpful when experienced in moderation. A person who feels a little angry, or tense or stressed or worried, may be able to channel that negativity to achieve precisely the result he or she is looking for. But over-the-top levels of these feelings impede the doing of anything at all.

Is there anywhere that extreme optimists have an edge? In personal life, they excel in certain social situations. They have an edge when it comes to maintaining close friendships and dating. That's great in life outside the office, but not so great at work. We all know people who socialize so much that they never seem to get anything done. That's the kind of thing that can hold you back when upper management notices.

Perhaps More Than Any Other Attribute, Optimism Is Connected to Differences

As you read through the chapters that follow (and the ones that came before), you'll find that the boundaries that separate some of the elements that make up The Difference are a bit, well, squishy. One attribute tends to beget the next, which leads to another, which happens to be tied to the first one. This is more true of optimism and happiness than perhaps any of the others.

PERCENT THAT FEELS EXTREMELY SATISFIED WITH THE FOLLOWING			
	Family Life	**Social Life**	**Health**
Wealthy	58 percent	46 percent	54 percent
Financially comfortable	54 percent	38 percent	37 percent
Paycheck-to-paychecks	42 percent	24 percent	21 percent
Further-in-debtors	27 percent	13 percent	15 percent

- Researchers have found optimism breeds connectedness. (See chapter 8.) Happy, optimistic people are more involved in their communities and have better social relationships than their more morose peers. And they are more satisfied with their friends and their extracurricular activities.

- They are higher in energy. Optimists simply *do* more. That enables them to accomplish more in their chosen line of work as well as in life outside of it. (See chapter 10.)

- "Doing more" includes pursuing personal—and financial—goals. As my research for *The Ten Commandments of Financial Happiness* documented, it's not just achieving the goal that leads to feelings of satisfaction, making progress toward it does, too. (See chapter 2.)

- Optimistic people are more likable than their less optimistic peers. That helps them attract mentors and others who will help them in their careers. (See chapter 3.)

- Happy people show a greater interest in helping others—whether through charitable efforts or social ones. They're more likely to spend some of their time shopping for a sick friend, helping a colleague at work or in school, or volunteering for their community. (See chapter 9.)

- Optimistic folks are resilient. Their coping mechanisms are more effective and more mature than those of people who aren't as positively inclined. (See chapter 6.)

- Likewise, optimistic people tend to be flexible thinkers. If their first try at a problem or puzzle doesn't work, they tend to be relaxed and creative enough to find the answer another way. (See chapter 3.)

Where Do You Stack Up?

For the past few decades, academics have used the Life Orientation Test to measure optimism. It was developed by Michael F. Schier, department head and professor of psychology at Carnegie Mellon University, and Charles S. Carver, distinguished professor of psychology at the University of Miami. Frederick G. Crane, executive professor of entrepreneurship and innovation at the Northeastern University College of Business Administration, first shared the revised version with me.

I took the test. He scored it, then taught me how to do it myself. Now it's your turn.

The Life Orientation Test

Place the appropriate number, 0, 1, 2, 3, or 4, next to each statement listed below to indicate the extent to which you agree or disagree with the statement. Please be as honest and accurate as you can throughout. Try not to let your response to one statement influence your responses to other statements. There are no "correct" or "incorrect" answers. Answer according to your own feelings, rather than how you think "most people" would answer.

0 = Strongly disagree

1 = Disagree

2 = You are neutral about the statement

3 = Agree

4 = Strongly agree

1. In uncertain times, I would expect the best.

2. It's easy for me to relax.

3. If something can go wrong with me, it will.

4. I am always optimistic about my future.

5. I enjoy my friends a lot.

6. It's important for me to keep busy.

7. I hardly ever expect things to go my way.

8. I don't get upset too easily.

9. I rarely count on good things happening to me.

10. Overall, I expect more good things to happen to me than bad.

To score: Items 2, 5, 6, and 8 are fillers. Don't count them at all. Score numbers 1, 4, and 10 according to the scale. Score numbers 3, 7, and 9 in reverse: 0 = 4; 1 = 3; 2 = 2; 3 = 1; and 4 = 0. Then add up your numbers. The higher your score, the more optimistic you are, with a breakdown that looks roughly like this:

> *Optimistic 20–24*
> *Mildly optimistic 14–19*
> *Neutral 11–13*
> *Mildly pessimistic 6–10*
> *Pessimistic 0–5*

You may be looking at these results and thinking: "So what? I was born this way. There is nothing I can do about it." That is decidedly untrue. Only about 50 percent of optimism and happiness is innate, which means that achieving an optimistic outlook is distinctly possible.

Also, starting from pessimistic can mean you'll see bigger financial improvements than if you start from neutral. The lower you are on the scale, the more improvements will mean to your bottom line. For example, a grumpy person who becomes moderately happy is likely to see a bigger boost in income than a happy person who becomes happier. So—get to it and get (at least a little) happy!

What If You Feel Too Happy or Optimistic?

CHALLENGE YOURSELF. One factor at work here is a hidden con of happiness. While positive emotions tend to make you more expansive and creative, they also make you rely on tried-and-true answers. The solution is to challenge yourself to find new and interesting solutions while the old ones are still working. How? Put yourself on a new committee at work. Take up a challenging sport or hobby. Do something (anything) that scares you.

AUTOMATE GOOD HABITS. Technology, thankfully, can fill the gaps when the optimist in you starts to overtake your good sense. Automate savings wherever you can: in your 401(k) plan (sign up for automatic escalation if it's offered), your IRA, your 529, and your savings account. And maintain a good balance in your investments using life-cycle or target-date mutual funds.

COVER YOUR BASES. Stop assuming everything will be fine in the end. If you don't have a will, living will, health-care proxy, life insurance, or disability insurance—and you know you need those things—this may very well explain why you haven't stepped up to the plate. Use this as a little nudge to get your inner pessimist to take a swing.

START A BUSINESS. Dave Thomas. Lillian Vernon. Stephen Covey. Earl Graves. Some of the country's best-known entrepreneurs—and many of those who are successful but not famous—self-report high levels of optimism. It's such a driving trait that Northeastern's Frederick Crane muses, "If you don't have this trait, starting a business is not a particularly good idea. Why? You won't be able to weather the inevitable ups and downs."

What If You're Not Happy or Optimistic Enough?

PRIORITIZE DOING, NOT ACQUIRING. We know, again from the research, that spending money on experiences makes people happier than spending money on things. The reason: Things pale over time. They lose their shine, their trendiness, their new-car smell. Experiences, on the other hand, get better in the retelling. Whether or not you embellish (and most people do) you get the same lift in sharing the story of how your horse broke away from the pack on the trail into the

Grand Canyon and how—despite the fact that you had never been on a horse before—you were able to rein it in, all by yourself.

LEARN TO SAVOR. Have you ever been in a car, driving along the highway, when you suddenly look up and wonder, how did I get here? You don't recall passing the last couple of exits. You can't remember what song just played on the radio. You took a mental holiday. On the road, of course, that's dangerous. In life, it's one of the things that reduces the enjoyment you take in your work, your kids, your friends, your hobbies. Learn to be present and start to notice the good things that are happening around you. Start small: Taste your hamburger, don't just eat it. You don't have to stop what you're doing, just be mindful of your actions. Savor the beauty of the moment.

COMPARE AND CONTRAST FAVORABLY. We all measure ourselves, our surroundings, and our belongings to those of people around us. It's the American thing to do. But rather than doing it as most people do—by casting yourself and your accomplishments in a negative light—choose your comparative set so that you come out looking good. You're not the least flexible one in your advanced yoga class. You're the most flexible one among the beginners. You're not the least successful person on your block, you're among the 10 percent most successful in your subdivision. If you catch yourself comparing down—and you will—force yourself to go back and find a more positive example. Over time, it will become second nature.

BECOME A LAWYER OR FILM CRITIC. Okay, I'm being a little facetious. But one way to strike a balance that works in your favor is to simply find something to do where your natural pessimism works in your favor. Psychology professor Martin Seligman of the University of Pennsylvania studied law students at the University of Virginia. He pitted the optimists against the pessimists, and the pessimists won out. They were more likely to make law review, get better grades, and get better job offers. Why? Common sense says that in the field of law, pessimism (and its cousin, skepticism) work to your advantage.

Why Getting Older Is Not Such a Bad Thing, Part I

I realize that I am not the only person on the planet who had trouble turning forty. And as fifty grows closer each year, let me just say I'm not looking forward to that one either.

As far as optimism and happiness are concerned, however, age is a good thing. What we're learning from medical research is that as you get older, your neurons or gray matter—the information processors and the part of your brain that makes you "neurotic"—start shrinking. The flip side is that the white matter—the insulated nerve fibers that connect neurons to one another and keep them working in tip-top order—keep growing. They peak anywhere from age forty-five to sixty, according to research from UCLA doctor George Bartzokis. You become a better multitasker and better at suppressing negative thoughts and letting positive ones emerge.

You also become more emotionally stable. Australian researcher Leanne Williams, director of the Brain Dynamics Centre at the Westmead Hospital at the University of Sydney, says that adults in middle age and older are better at regulating their emotions. So they find themselves in a positive state of mind more of the time and in a bad mood less often. Women, interestingly enough, seem to be better emotional regulators than men.

More Good News—Once You Find Optimism, You're Likely to Keep It

Here's one final motivating factor to get you to try to increase your levels of both optimism and happiness, if that's what you need to do. For years, the world of positive psychology was stuck on a concept called "the hedonic treadmill." Conceived by the University of Illinois's Ed

Diener and Nobel Prize winner Daniel Kahneman of Princeton, this essentially said no matter what you do to try to improve your happiness, to raise your level of optimism, you will always go back to your baseline. In 2006, Diener published a paper in *American Psychologist* in which it was clear he was stepping back from that notion. By the following year, he was calling it a mistake.

This is, by the way, how science works. A notion is posited. It is proven. Sometimes it is disproven later. In this particular case, this is good news, because it means that work that you do on yourself will not be in vain. You can achieve long-lasting results. You don't have to keep going to the mental gym.

Exercise: Write About the Very Best You

In 2006, researchers at the University of Missouri undertook an experiment on sixty-seven psychology students. To begin, the students were asked to take a mood questionnaire, which they repeated two weeks into the study and again at four weeks. Then, once a week for the next four weeks, they were asked to consider—and write about—the very best versions of themselves. They were told, "If the road rose up to meet you at every turn for the next five, ten, fifteen years, what goals would you have accomplished, what dreams would you have achieved? What would your ideal life look like in the future if you could spell it out for yourself? This is the scenario I want you to think about. You're doing this exercise because research has shown that thinking about your future life in the best possible terms is likely to have a good influence on the decisions that you make, as well as your current outlook on life."

Another group of students was put through similar paces, but they were asked to write about the state of their lives now: what a typical day was like, how they felt about it, and so on. Both groups were encouraged to keep going with the exercise for at least a month. Then the groups were compared. What happened? Both groups experienced reductions in negativity, but the reduction in the group envisioning their best possible life was much greater. Additionally, the students in the best possible life group were more likely to say they identified with the exercise, that it fit with their values, and that they were more likely to continue doing it.

So that's your exercise. Once a week for the next four weeks consider the very best version of yourself. You'll basically be keeping a very positive journal. As you go through the process, use positive terms to explain your actions. Don't write: "I can't afford to live in the city, so I live in the suburbs." Write: "I live in the suburbs rather than the city because I choose to spend my money on other things." Remember, on these pages you are not a victim, you are in charge. As a jump start, you can fill in these blanks.

TODAY I AM:

   I GOT HERE BY:

FIVE YEARS FROM NOW I WILL BE:

   I GOT THERE BY:

TEN YEARS FROM NOW I WILL BE:

   I GOT THERE BY:

TWENTY YEARS FROM NOW I WILL BE:

   I GOT THERE BY:

I AM MOST PROUD OF:

Note: It's fine if you come up with several best possible scenarios. This exercise helps you establish priorities, gives insight into what you really want, and shines a light on your motivations and values. By doing it repeatedly, you see what items are flashes in the pan and which show up week after week. Seeing yourself in the form of the person you'd like to be also improves your chances of becoming that person.

A Quick Guide to Chapter 6

By any conventional measure, a mere seven years after my gradu-
ation day, I had failed on an epic scale. An exceptionally short-
lived marriage had imploded, and I was jobless, a lone parent,
and as poor as it is possible to be. . . . I was the biggest failure I
knew. Why do I talk about the benefits of failure? Simply because
failure meant a stripping away of the inessential. I stopped pre-
tending to myself that I was anything other than what I was and
began to direct all my energy into finishing the only work that
mattered to me. Had I really succeeded at anything else, I might
never have found the determination to succeed in the one arena I
believed I truly belonged.

I take great heart in that passage—from J. K. Rowling's commence-
ment address at Harvard in 2008. And it's not because I'm a Harry
Potter fan (which I am). It's because I think it's a perfect illustration of
resilience—the ability to pick yourself up, dust yourself off, and, as the
song says, start all over again. And resilience is a key element in The
Difference. Everybody fails, occasionally. Some people more than
that. And even if what doesn't kill you doesn't necessarily make you
stronger, it does seem to give you a leg up on wealth.

In this chapter, you'll meet a man who credits overcoming a huge
obstacle in his early teens with his business success later in life. You'll
take a test to learn where your greatest coping skills lie—and then use
that information to hone your strengths and beef up your weaknesses.
And at the end, I'll provide another exercise to incorporate into your
life. Are you feeling The Difference yet?

MEET NORRIS

AGE: Sixty-seven
FAMILY: Married, two children
ASSETS: $2 million to $3 million
NORRIS'S DIFFERENCES: Grateful, resilient, intuitive, takes risks

Some people are born knowing that they have the ability to accomplish precisely what they want to accomplish. From the time they head into grade school they are knocking down roadblocks, meeting expectations, dreaming big. For others, like Norris, the ability to rise to the top remained hidden—until something unleashed the power within.

Q: How'd you get your start?

A: I went into business for myself back in the '70s as an automobile dealer about forty miles west of Atlanta. I went into a partnership for a short time and then, about a year and a half later, I bought the business. For fifteen years, from the time I was thirty-five until I was fifty, I sold Chevrolets.

Q: And after that?

A: I sold the business. I haven't had a job in eighteen years. Since then, I've pretty much been a man of leisure. It's not a bad way to live, I enjoy retirement. I got bored one time so I went to college for three and a half years. That was something I always wanted to do and I enjoyed it. It's a lot of fun when you're older than all the teachers—they listen to you. I consider myself very fortunate.

Q: But it also sounds like you worked very hard?

A: [Chuckling.] I put a little effort into it. Times change. But back when I went into the car business—and this is my opinion—the only thing you had to do to be successful was to be honest. And work hard. That business, as you well know, has a stigma to it, because not everybody in it is honest. So that was my philosophy. Be a man of your word. I felt strongly about it, and so every car I sold, whether it was a brand-new one or a used clunker for $100, I guaranteed it. But I think when a person spends their hard-earned money for something, the only way you can give people value is treat them right and back up what you sell.

Q: You mean you would take that $100 car back if something went wrong?

A: That's what I lived by. If I sold you a vehicle and I guaranteed it to be good and it wasn't, last resort—I don't think I did this but once or twice—I give you your money back. If I give you your money back, you gotta say good things about me. That was important to me. I was forty miles from Atlanta. If I could get someone from Atlanta to come out and give me their business, I knew I had them locked from then on.

Q: How has business changed since then?

A: I know a lot of younger people—I have two grown daughters of my own. Both are dedicated to their work and they work hard. But younger people want to enjoy things now, not in the future. It was different from me. I felt like I had to save money, and I poured it all back into the business.

Q: No CDs, no stocks?

A: During the period I'm talking about, you could get 10, 12, 15 percent in the bank. But I don't think I ever had a year that I didn't earn 20 percent on my investment.

Q: Didn't it frighten you to put all your eggs in that one basket?

A: Today I would be terrified. But I think that's because I'm sixty-seven years old. When I was thirty-seven, nothing frightened me. In fact, now it's a joke in the neighborhood. I don't fly anymore because I'm scared to fly. Back then, I felt like as long as I was in control, I'd do fine with my finances.

Q: I need to stick with this for a second. You were the primary wage earner with two young children and you didn't feel like you were taking an awful lot of risk?

A: When I bought the business from my partner, it cost sixty grand and I was worth about $10. But it didn't make me nervous, I felt like it was a heck of a good deal. I felt I would be successful. I had a gut feeling. I hit the auto business at its very bottom. That was luck—some things can only get so bad. Then we had four years of Jimmy Carter. That wasn't easy.

Q: Four years would send a lot of people to the poorhouse. What made you so invincible, so confident?

A: Confident? Well, this is a crazy story. I was born in 1940. Things have changed a lot since then, but from the time I was born until I was twelve years old, I had a vision problem. I couldn't see very well. And, well, I grew up in a small town. Maybe we didn't have adequate people to correct it. Well, at twelve I had it corrected. Let me tell you, I was a lousy athlete at twelve and a pretty damn good one at thirteen. And I think that was because I could see. When you step up to the plate and strike out—that makes you doubt yourself. When you step up to the plate and hit it out of the park, you feel like you can do just about anything.

Q: You're happy.
A: I am happy. I think that's what success is about.

Q: And you clearly have money, but you didn't describe yourself as wealthy.

A: I haven't got $5 million. But I could write you a check for $2 [million]. My gosh. That's not wealthy. I think I would feel wealthy if I had $12 to $15 million in assets. I think I would. Of course, when I was a kid, I thought if I ever made $100 bucks a week, I'd be pretty well-off.

CHAPTER SIX

In Praise of the Do-Over

In this world, as you well know, things happen. It rains when you want to play tennis. You get fired from a job you like. You have to sit on a runway for four hours while they inspect the plane's fuselage. Your parents get divorced. Your dog dies. Gas prices go to $4 a gallon two months after you buy an SUV. Things happen.

So what can you do? You can cave in to these events, some of which you can control a little, some of which you cannot control at all. Or you can learn to deal, ride it out, and come to terms with the fact that things will take care of themselves in time.

This is called "resilience." It's not a new word, by any means, but it does seem to have been reinvigorated lately by both the media and academics. That makes sense, considering the definition, which, according to Merriam-Webster, is "an ability to recover from or adjust easily to misfortune or change." It sounds like a dose of *precisely* what we need right now.

Resilient people keep moving forward. They don't get stuck in a pool of negativity. They don't deny the bad things that happen in all of our lives, but they focus on things they can control. They believe they can affect change.

Resilience is not a single skill. It's made up of a variety of skills—of coping mechanisms—and these tactics (some conscious, others not so much) operate along a continuum. Think of the times you've had set-backs in your life. Some you've handled with such ease or aplomb you might have wondered who that poised stranger inhabiting your body was. Recalling others, you're still embarrassed because you acted like a three-year-old. And there are many other times and moments some-where in between.

People who know The Difference are resilient.

"I can overcome a bad situation."

	Percent That Agree
Wealthy	49 percent
Financially comfortable	51 percent
Paycheck-to-paychecks	40 percent
Further-in-debtors	37 percent

"I always finish what I start."

	Percent That Agree
Wealthy	41 percent
Financially comfortable	38 percent
Paycheck-to-paychecks	30 percent
Further-in-debtors	32 percent

Being resilient is a key factor for our movers as well.

Attribute	Describes Me	Percent More Likely to Move Forward Than Those Who Said the Word Didn't Describe Them At All
Resilient	Slightly	14 percent
	Well	27 percent
	Very well	34 percent
	Completely	26 percent

Luckily—like optimism, gratitude, and other important factors that make up The Difference—resilience is not something you have to be born with, says Dr. Karen Reivich, co-author of *The Resilience Factor: Seven Essential Skills for Overcoming Life's Inevitable Obstacles* and codirector of the Penn Resiliency Program at the University of Pennsylvania. That wasn't her initial perception. "I thought I'd learn that resilience was something hardwired," she admits. "But that's absolutely false. Some people are more naturally resilient, it's true, but what our research shows is that almost anyone can increase their resilience by learning a set of skills."

How Do You Cope?

That's the first question. We do it in different ways at different times. Psychologist Charles S. Carver of the University of Miami has designed a diagnostic test called COPE. What follows is his brief version, edited slightly for these purposes. (His longer version is available at his website, www.psy.miami.edu/faculty/ccarver, under "Current Projects and Interests.")

Use this scale as you go through the following questions.

1 = I haven't been doing this at all.
2 = I've been doing this a little bit.

3 = *I've been doing this a medium amount.*
4 = *I've been doing this a lot.*

Answer the questions quickly and honestly, paying close attention to what extent you've been doing what each item says. You want to gauge how often or how much you've been doing this, not whether it seems to be working for you. Try to approach each question individually, as distinct and separate from the others.

This is not a test of whether you're resilient or not. Instead, you'll see which coping mechanisms you are using most often, which will help you make better use of this chapter.

1. I've been turning to work or other activities to take my mind off things.

2. I've been concentrating my efforts on doing something about the situation I'm in.

3. I've been saying to myself "This isn't real."

4. I've been using alcohol or other drugs to make myself feel better.

5. I've been getting emotional support from others.

6. I've been giving up trying to deal with it.

7. I've been taking action to try to make the situation better.

8. I've been refusing to believe that it has happened.

9. I've been saying things to let my unpleasant feelings escape.

10. I've been getting help and advice from other people.

11. I've been using alcohol or other drugs to help me get through it.

12. I've been trying to see it in a different light, to make it seem more positive.

13. I've been criticizing myself.

14. I've been trying to come up with a strategy about what to do.

15. I've been getting comfort and understanding from someone.

16. I've been giving up on the attempt to cope.

17. I've been looking for something good in what is happening.

18. I've been making jokes about it.

19. I've been doing something to think about it less, such as going to movies, watching TV, reading, daydreaming, sleeping, or shopping.

20. I've been accepting the reality of the fact that it has happened.

21. I've been expressing my negative feelings.

22. I've been trying to find comfort in my religion or spiritual beliefs.

23. I've been trying to get advice or help from other people about what to do.

24. I've been learning to live with it.

25. I've been thinking hard about what steps to take.

26. I've been blaming myself for things that happened.

27. I've been praying or meditating.

28. I've been making fun of the situation.

Scoring: Use the following key to figure out which coping measures you're using a lot (you answered 3 or 4) and which ones you're not using very much (you answered 1 or 2). Next, we'll discuss the methods you can use to help yourself become more resilient.

Questions 1, 19: Self-distraction
2, 7: Active coping
3, 8: Denial

4, 11: Substance use

5, 15: Use of emotional support

10, 23: Use of instrumental support

6, 16: Behavioral disengagement

9, 21: Venting

12, 17: Positive reframing

14, 25: Planning

18, 28: Humor

20, 24: Acceptance

22, 27: Spirituality or religion

13, 26: Self-blame

The M-Word Rears Its Head (Again)

There are some items on the above list that many people immediately read as negative: Substance use. Denial. Self-blame. Yet, as Harvard Medical School psychologist Robert Brooks, coauthor of *The Power of Resilience: Achieving Balance, Confidence, and Personal Strength in Your Life*, notes, they can actually work in your favor at times. A small amount of denial can enable you to continue to work on a problem instead of quitting, giving you sufficient time to conquer it. A modest amount of self-blame may be what's needed to get you to face the truth. As for substance use—as long as it doesn't turn into abuse, who can argue it? (As I write this, a substance found in red wine is in the news as the potential fountain of youth!) Too much of any of these things, however, and you turn the tide.

The same is true with the more positive-sounding coping strategies on the list. Humor is great. Until it becomes sarcasm. Venting is fine—and sometimes necessary—as long as you're taking out your frustrations in your journal or on a punching bag, rather than on an actual person. Finding solace in spirituality or faith is fantastic, until you find yourself spending more time meditating than actually doing.

Increasing Your RQ (Resilience Quotient)

On the next few pages, we'll talk about different things you can do to improve your coping ability. You'll note that not every form of coping is on this list of learnable skills. Humor, for instance, isn't there—not because there aren't plenty of resilient people whose wicked sense of humor is their go-to strength, but because it isn't teachable. Don't worry. There are plenty of others to choose from.

Some will fit the way you see the world, and you'll be able to easily incorporate them into your thinking. Others may seem so straightforward you can cross them off your list; these are things you do already. And, finally, there will be those that—to you—are akin to an orange sweater (and you don't wear orange) or steak tartare (and you like your meat well done). That's okay, too. Not all strategies work for all people; that's why so many exist.

Eleven Coping Strategies for You to Try

ASK YOURSELF ONE QUESTION. Do I have to change or does someone else have to change for me to succeed at this? Here's the deal: Resilient people identify and then focus on the things they have control over, rather than try to change things over which they don't. Other people, for example. If getting your significant other to wake up early in the morning on weekends is the challenge and he or she has always valued that catch-up sleep, you're fighting a losing battle. Perhaps you can find something you'd like to do solo in those hours instead. It's a method that works brilliantly when other people are your foil—because essentially it means we are taking responsibility for our own lives rather than blaming someone else for them—but it's not limited to other people. What if the thing out of your control is the stock market? You cannot control (or predict, but that's another story) whether it goes up or down on a particular day, week, month, or year. But you can control how much you decide to put in stocks rather than bonds; how seriously you take asset allocation and diversification; whether you decide to look at your portfolio on a daily, weekly, or even quarterly basis, and how you respond to it when you do.

DO SOMETHING. It may be the wrong thing. That's okay, you'll do something else later. If you're ignoring the problem or dwelling on the negative—which can happen without your realizing it, although your answers to questions 8, 13, 16, and 19 are signs—you may not be trying to solve your problems because you don't know where to start. Acknowledge that there is an issue—that things at work, in your relationship, with your money, wherever, aren't the way you want them to be. Then brainstorm two or three possible solutions to the problem. Pick one. (If you can't decide which one, I'll pick for you. Number one.) And go about implementing it. Just like exercising frees your mind to explore other options, taking action when you're stuck—even if it's a wrongheaded, inefficient action—can get you moving in some direction. You'll find the right direction later.

TAKE A BREAK. This is the opposite of doing something, although for some people action is involved. If you are at work on a challenge or immersed in a project, and it is going nowhere, stop. Sometimes what your mind needs is a break to clear itself, to recharge the batteries, so that it can move forward again. This is why sleep is regenerative. But sleeping isn't the only break that works. Try taking a walk or a jog. Listening to music that moves you. Or baking a cake. Or even consider wallowing for a bit. Think Holly Hunter in *Broadcast News*. She set her alarm clock for a good fifteen-minute daily cry. Christopher Reeve did the same thing in the years following his accident. He allowed himself twenty minutes to cry or dwell on how life was before. And when it was over, he got on with his day.

FIND A CHEERLEADER. For his book *Startups That Work: The Ten Critical Factors That Will Make or Break a New Company* Joel Kurtzman evaluated 350 start-ups (and starting a company is an exercise requiring resilience if I've ever heard one). He found that when two or three people share an idea of what they're striving for, their chances of success hit 50 percent. For people on their own, it was 10 percent. This is not to say that you need someone working with you to scale your mountains. But you do need someone who believes that you can do it. Brooks's resiliency research proves that notion. Linda Meccouri concurs. Meccouri, a professor at Springfield Technical Community College in Massachusetts, was raised in poverty. She says, "This Horatio Alger story, that you can raise yourself up by your boot-straps, is a myth." Meccouri has spent the last twenty-six years taking oral histories of people, primarily women, who have escaped poverty and found financial comfort. She says her subjects—to a one—have said, "There's a person in my life. An ally. A mentor." Meccouri has taken to calling these people "healers."

"We were broke or damaged and these people—the teacher who kept the kid after school in second grade and asked her to help water the plants—healed us."

DO IT FOR SOMEONE ELSE. This leads to another strategy. There are times you simply cannot be resilient for yourself. Why? You don't feel as if you're worth it. That child in second grade very likely didn't water her plants at home—if there were any plants to water. But she could do it for her teacher. And there will be times when you may not feel able to scale that mountain for yourself, but perhaps you can do it for your child, parent, or spouse, or that teacher who believed in you long ago.

EMPHASIZE THE POSITIVE. We all know someone who just dwells, dwells, and dwells some more on everything negative in life. Heck, we've probably all been there at one point or another our-selves. But part of being resilient is being optimistic, and so it's im-portant to find ways to put positive emotions in your day, says Karen Reivich. That means recognizing the good stuff that happens to you each day. Write it down, if that helps. "What we find is that when people make [noticing the good] a part of their daily routine, it increases their positive emotions, and that improves resilience," explains Reivich.

BE REALISTIC. A big part of being resilient, says Dr. Al Seibert, author of *The Resiliency Advantage: Master Change, Thrive Under Pressure, and Bounce Back from Setbacks,* is flat-out asking yourself: "Do I really need to be concerned about this?" If you have your money in the market through a 401(k) or an IRA, and every time you check your balance it's a little bit lower and a little bit lower, it's easy to get worked up, I know. And sure, you could pull out, but then you risk missing out on some great returns once the market bounces back. Where your money is concerned, you are not always going to win, so you have to be able to stomach the ups and downs of the market. Turn off CNBC, take a walk, stop reading the business section of the paper, see a movie—do whatever it takes to get your mind off your money for a while.

SILENCE YOUR INTERNAL CRITICS. "People who have this very harsh internal radio station that plays nothing but negativity over and over again find it very difficult to reach their goals, succeed at work, and build strong relationships," says Reivich. You might expect her to advise you to tune it out, but that's not the best way to deal. Instead, turn the volume up so you can hear the negative thoughts loud enough that you can challenge them with evidence that shoots them down. If you were to accuse me of being lazy, I could rattle off evidence to prove to you that it's not true. But if I wake up and say the same thing, I act as if, because it came from my brain, it must be a fact. To undo that damage, come up with one piece of real evidence that refutes the point. One solid piece. Then allow your brain to build a case around that.

ACKNOWLEDGE YOUR GAFFES—AND MOVE ON. Of course, it's important to acknowledge when you make a mistake, but what you don't want to do is dwell on it. So, for example, if you're beating yourself up for spending too much at the mall yesterday, recognize that you screwed up, but then move on to solving the problem—maybe you move money around in your budget, return whatever you bought, or cut back on spending next week.

GET RID OF DISTRACTIONS. Remember solving word problems in grade school math? The teacher would make you underline the parts of the problem that really matter so that you could get rid of everything extraneous, of all the distractions. Well, unfortunately, today distractions are everywhere. E-mail. Voice mail. Television. The Internet. Meetings. It's amazing we ever get anything done, let alone anything challenging enough to require resilience. Research says that every time you turn away from the task at hand to, say, answer an e-mail, it takes fifteen minutes to reengage your brain in the initial challenge. So get rid of the distractions. Shut down the e-mail. Turn off the television. Unplug the phone. If need be, take yourself somewhere away from these things so that for a short while you can focus in peace.

LOOK INSIDE FOR YOUR WORTH. There was a time, Linda Meccouri recalls, about a decade ago, when her finances were in such bad shape that she had to move with her children into a trailer. "I never want to go back there," she says. "It's not okay with me to go back there. But I could do it then because I knew that wasn't my real value. Having a house, being in a house, wasn't my value. My value was my family and my children. So we sat there in that camper while they did their homework, while they practiced violin." Bravo. When listeners on my radio show call in when they're in a jam, I often tell them that they are not their credit scores. They are not the number on the page. If they believe that, then they are truly lost. I believe they—you—have the power to build those numbers, to shore up your financial security, to accomplish whatever it is you want for yourself. But it's not enough for me to believe it. You'll know you've mastered resilience when you believe it, too.

HABITS THAT HELP: EXERCISE

Just thirty minutes of exercise a day—even brisk walking is sufficient—is enough to increase blood flow to the brain. Exercise—because it's associated with the release of endorphins, which relieve pain and depression—can make you happier, less stressed and anxious, and give you a self-esteem boost. And that's before you get to all the physical benefits. But did you know that routine exercising is tied to wealth as well?

The wealthy people in our sample were much more likely to be regular exercisers than those lower on the economic scale.

"I exercise at least two to three times per week."

	Percent That Agreed
Wealthy	50 percent
Financially comfortable	41 percent
Paycheck-to-paychecks	26 percent
Further-in-debtors	23 percent

That's a result you might expect, based on the fact that the wealthy are better able to afford gym memberships and personal trainers, as well as the time away from work to do something good for themselves. But the results of our movers—the people who leaped from further in debt or living paycheck to paycheck into financial comfort and wealth, hammered home the finding.

Habit	Describes Me	Percent More Likely to Move Forward Than Those Who Said the Phrase Didn't Describe Them at All
Exercise two to three times per week	Slightly	8 percent
	Well	9 percent
	Very well	16 percent
	Completely	16 percent

Exercise is hugely important, said Duke's David Robinson, who helped analyze the data. People who exercise more frequently are the ones who are able to move upward in wealth. And those who don't exercise are just the opposite—more likely to slide back.

Resilience seems to be particularly well-linked to exercise. When you get moving, anxiety—which is often manifested physically—begins to quiet down. The parts of your brain sending messages about being overwhelmed tame themselves. Instead you start to hear, "I am okay. I can do this. I am in control."

What Happens When You Learn These Skills

Resilient people have the ability to take the appropriate risks necessary to embrace The Difference. They're more comfortable in uncomfortable situations. They can overcome pessimism. They can pull themselves out of minor depressions.

Why? Because resilience—learned resilience—gives humans the power to overcome our innate negativity. We appear to be hardwired to pay more attention to the bad things that happen than the good things. We dwell on them. We illuminate them. Becoming resilient requires more positive emotion, more optimism. (See chapter 5.) When people seek out the good stuff, it increases positive emotions, and that improves resilience. Think of it as filling up your positivity tank so that you have enough power to keep going when you're under stress and need it most.

Notes the University of Pennsylvania's Karen Reivich, who teaches resilience in the classroom, "When someone learns this skill, and in the heat of the moment is able to fight back and quiet that part of the brain, we see a complete shift. They stand taller, their energy changes, and they get more engaged in what they're doing."

In other words, you'll have the ability to see the world as it is, warts and all, solve the problems, and move on.

"If You Have to Cut Butter with a Chain Saw, Cut Butter with a Chain Saw."

If you read the financial pages or watch CNBC you may know Diane Swonk as the charismatic chief economist of Mesirow Financial. What you likely don't know is that she's the walking epitome of resilience. She grew up in Detroit, the daughter of a dyslexic father, and realized early on that she was also dyslexic. She's a single mother of two. And she was in the World Trade Center on September 11, 2001. "I had every belief I would live, and it was scary as hell," she recalls. "But I told myself, 'Now is not the time to panic. I will deal with the emotions later.' At the moment, when you are in a crisis you know how to handle it. You take care of yourself later."

The ability to be resourceful—to handle whatever crisis comes her way—is something she learned by dealing with dyslexia her entire life. "I think it defines who I am today," she says. "My father was dyslexic and ashamed of it. He didn't fit well in the Catholic school system. It was very hard to be a square peg in a round hole—that's how he saw himself. When I came of age, they were finally putting a name on it. So the mantra for me became 'If you have to cut butter with a chain saw, cut butter with a chain saw.' Figure out how to get it done."

And then, if you're able, use your differences—what other people may think of as your deficiencies—to rise above. "What dyslexia did was make me think outside the box. That nonlinear thinking is actually responsible for much of my success as an economist," she says. "People like me and Charles Schwab [also dyslexic], we get there first. We look at what other people see as chaos and see clarity."

For example: Swonk landed a job at First Chicago in September 1985. Her first assignment was to immerse herself in the Midwest economy. So she did. She looked at oil prices (which were falling), the dollar (which was depreciating), costs (which had been cut), and—though her competitors were all gloom and doom—she saw a very bright future. "All the things that put us under have reversed," she said at the time. "The 1990s are going to belong to us." People thought she was nuts, but Swonk wrote a big paper backing up her theory, and it helped shape the strategy that took First Chicago from a smallish bank to a financial force in the Midwest. (After several mergers and acquisitions, it is now part of JPMorgan Chase.)

Failure Is Not an Option (It's a Necessity)

What do you say to yourself when you screw up? Do you mutter "Idiot" under your breath? Or do you say something like, "That was not a smart thing to do"? The subtext is completely different. If you're an idiot, you couldn't help it. If you did a not-so-smart thing, you can change course and do it differently the next time. There's an old saying: "Only he who does nothing makes no mistakes." It's an important point. Resilience is not about not failing. It's about learning what to do better the next time.

In our survey, we asked a series of questions to get at the notion of what factors successful—and not so successful—people believe are holding them back. Here are the results:

Why are you not where you want to be?	
Don't have enough savings	19 percent
Income is not high enough	15 percent
Overdid it with debt	11 percent
Cost of living is too high	9 percent
Disability/unable to work	7 percent
Child/family-related expenses are greater than anticipated	5 percent
Lost a job	4 percent
Educational costs are higher than expected	4 percent
Inflation	4 percent

I find it interesting that most of these factors (except, perhaps, for inflation and disability) are things within our control. Asserting that control—as you'll learn in this chapter as well as those that follow on the saving, investing, and spending habits that make up The Difference—is completely within your power. You simply have to decide you're going to take the reins.

And there's no better time than when you're feeling low to make that change. Why? Because from the bottom, anywhere you go will be an improvement. Anywhere you go from there will be up. Sir John Templeton used that theory—what he called "the point of maximum pessimism"—to drive his very successful investments. When things look the worst, he often explained, that's when you have the greatest opportunity for returns in the markets. It's also when you have the greatest opportunities to make a splash in life.

Don't believe me? There are plenty of famous examples. Michael Jordan was cut from his high school basketball team. Dozens of record companies rejected the Beatles and told them their sound was awful. CNN told Katie Couric that she'd never be allowed on the air again. More than one hundred publishers passed on the proposal for *Chicken Soup for the Soul* by Jack Canfield and Mark Victor Hanson. The examples go on and on and on. And it all comes back to what Thomas Edison said when asked by a *New York Times* reporter if he felt like a failure after hundreds of unsuccessful attempts to make a lightbulb. "I have not failed seven hundred times," Edison is said to have responded. "I have not failed once. I have succeeded in proving that those seven hundred ways will not work. When I have eliminated the ways that will not work, I will find the way that will work."

You learn. Persist. Adapt. Don't do the same thing over and over again. In the words of *Project Runway*'s Tim Gunn, do what you have to do to "make it work."

Exercise: Learn to Recast Your Experiences

New research tells us that it's better for our resilience to retell our life stories in such a way that it bolsters our confidence rather than weakens it. How do you do that?

TELL YOUR STORY IN THE THIRD PERSON. If I were doing it, I would talk about Jean. "Jean was on television this morning and it went . . ." "Jean threw a dinner party last night and . . ." This gives you the ability to step back and be impartial, and allows you to figure out why you behaved and felt as you did. Pay close attention to whether you make it seem like things happened to you or whether you made things happen. The former tends to victimize you, the latter to make you stronger next time.

LOOK AT THE POSITIVES YOU GOT FROM THE NEGATIVES. If you gloss over the unpleasant experiences in your retelling, you don't give yourself the opportunity to learn from them. Delve into them in a detailed way. Then spend time explaining—to yourself—how you're in a better place because you went through these challenges. You may not even realize these hidden benefits until you explain them out loud.

Exercise: Put It in Perspective

When adversity strikes a person who is not resilient, he or she will start to turn it into a catastrophe. To spin the story, like James Carville on speed. "If I can't pay my credit card bill this month then . . ." it might begin. But the ending is inevitable. "The world stops spinning and nothing will be right ever, ever again." A resilient person can stop the madness.

And this, too, is a skill you can learn. Take out a piece of paper and write down your catastrophic beliefs, your worst-case scenarios. For some of you that list will be ten items long, for others fifty. Then challenge those items by constructing an equally likely best-case scenario. Come up with the positive side, the fantasy. It may be difficult—actually, it probably will be to start—but once you get with the game, it can be playful and fun.

An example: "I'm going to lose my job."

Catastrophe: My girlfriend will dump me. My dog will hate me. I will end up eating out of a Dumpster.

Fantasy: Tomorrow I'll discover the cure for cancer. Someone will give me my own talk show. I'll win the lottery, even though I don't play.

What you start to see is that neither scenario is reality based. It just shows what's happening in your brain. When you're thinking pessimistically, your creativity narrows and your problem-solving abilities fade. So now that you're loosened up, do the hard work and look at the reality.

Reality: I'm going to have to redo my résumé. Each day I can make five or ten networking calls. It'll probably take me three or four months to land something good. I have savings I can live on if I don't spend like a crazy person.

A Quick Guide to Chapter 7

Are you a risk taker? Not an airplane-jumping, mountain-scaling, extreme-sport kind of risk taker. A taker of calculated risks—at work, in investing, in relationships, in life. This sort of risk taking (with a boost from better-than-average intuition) turns out to be an important part of The Difference. In the pages that follow, you'll learn why you perceive certain situations as riskier than others, how to fine-tune your perspective, and why optimism may not play the role you think.

MEET RANDY

AGE: Sixty-two
FAMILY: Three children
ASSETS: $1 million to $2.5 million
RANDY'S DIFFERENCES: Takes risks, grateful, resilient, able to read other people, hardworking

One way to cut the risk in any situation is to know what that situation is all about. That has been Randy's approach to risk taking. Throughout his life he has borrowed millions of dollars, taken options for pay in lieu of actual cash, and ventured into troubled companies in hopes of turning them around. He couched all of these risks by knowing precisely what he was doing. As he says, "Life just isn't as complicated as people make it for themselves."

Q: *I'm going to dive right in. So, how did you get financially comfortable?*

A: The simplest way to articulate my philosophy is to say that I prepared myself educationally, I was willing to take risks, and I was in the right place at the right time.

Q: *What's your educational background?*

A: I have a BS in accounting, master's degree in health administration, and a CPA.

Q: How were you a risk taker?

A: Over the years, I had to borrow [millions of dollars] at the bank. I had to be willing to sacrifice salary for amounts later to come, based on my efforts and success in the business world. Rather than taking a comfortable job that pays the same every month, I took less money and stock options.

Q: In other words, you bet on yourself.

A: I am a medical entrepreneur and I have been in several different parts of the medical business over the past thirty-five years. First, I was a hospital administrator. Next, I worked for a public health-care company where employees received stock options—that was my first taste of financial success. My big score was in the medical lab business. I ran a reference lab where all the physicians and hospitals sent lab work that couldn't be done in the office or hospital.

Q: Forgive my ignorance, but I'm not sure I know what a reference lab is.

A: It's basically a big outside lab. A reference lab affords economies of scale to buy larger equipment and to hire higher level PhDs. I was president and chief operating officer of that company. I worked with twenty-five pathologists. When I started there, the lab was owned by somebody else, and I was hired to improve it. The pathologists wanted to purchase the company from the owner. So I negotiated and borrowed quite a bit of money to buy the lab. At that time, ten of us signed on the dotted line for a million each. We began to grow by acquiring and merging with other labs that had only one or two pathologists. We grew the company from $8 million to $55 million in sales over eight years. We sold the lab after an eight-year run. I guess that's where I became financially comfortable.

Q: Wow. So what happened next?

A: I helped get a company in South Carolina stabilized. We sold it to a Chicago company. We swapped stock. I didn't have a lot of equity, but I did have some. Much later, five years, that company got bought and I got a bit of equity out of that. After that, I worked for an investment firm evaluating deals for them. I even worked for HealthSouth—before the scandal—for a little while.

Q: And now?

A: I work for a company that staffs emergency rooms for hospitals and urgent-care centers.

Q: Now, a lot of folks don't feel comfortable bragging, but I want you to tell me why you've succeeded and the next guy didn't.

A: In addition to being willing to take risks, I try to simplify things. Life just isn't as complicated as people make it for themselves. My greatest strength over the years in business has been interviewing and selecting people who had the same entrepreneurial spirit as I did. They don't give up. They don't expect something without working for it. But I haven't done it by myself. In the medical lab, we had close to one thousand employees. When I'm interviewing a person who starts to say, "I did this, then I did this, and guess what, I did this," I get worried. If they don't say they were surrounded by good people, I get worried. You always have to surround yourself with smart people—some of them smarter than you.

CHAPTER SEVEN

Taking Risks That Make Sense

Have you ever wanted to do something—try a new sport, new career, new diet, buy a new mutual fund—but haven't been able to pull the trigger? It can be frustrating—often because you're wondering why you can't do it.

It's called risk. When you change the status quo, even a little bit, it puts you and your body, career, ego, money, relationship, or some other facet of your life, on the line. You could fail. You could succeed. And, believe it or not, you may be afraid of both.

Let's deal with the less surprising first: fear of failure. If you're afraid of failing, you don't want to act because you're afraid of being wrong, being outed as a fraud, or looking like a fool. "It's the thing that traps people most," says psychologist Mort Harmatz of the University of Massachusetts, who has dealt with this for many decades in the classroom and in clinical practice. "It's why employees can't ask for a raise and why graduate students can't finish their doctorates."

And it's particularly problematic because in this scenario, inaction—not doing anything—is preferable to action. If you don't do anything, if you don't step up to the plate, you cannot make a mistake.

And in the heads of many people, that is much better than trying and failing.

The other fear—that of success—is a little more difficult to decipher. On the face of it, you wouldn't think that it would even be an issue. But think about what happens if you lose a lot of weight or gain a lot of wealth. Some people in your life are happy for you. Others are envious or resentful. Perhaps your heavier friends don't want to eat out with you on your new vegan diet, or your colleagues don't want to hang out unless you're grabbing the check. Even your siblings might be troubled that you conquered mountains they had been unable to scale. Subconsciously, you suspect that all of these things might happen. So even while you're talking a good game about wanting to get rich or thin, a little voice in the back of your mind is pumping the brakes.

Risk in the World of Finance

In the world of money, risk becomes even more nuanced. For many years, economists operated on a notion introduced in 1738, by Swiss mathematician Daniel Bernoulli, that people make financial decisions based on their perception of how wealthy the outcome might make them. It took a psychologist, Nobel laureate Daniel Kahneman, to prove that theory wrong. People don't think about their overall wealth, he argued. They think about gains and losses, which is different.

To understand why, consider this classic Kahneman example: Two people get their quarterly 401(k) statements. One learns that his balance has climbed from $1 million to $1.2 million. The other learns that his wealth has dropped from $4 million to $3.5 million. According to classic Bernoulli theory, the only thing that matters in the end is who is better off. Who has the most wealth? And that, of course, is the second individual.

But Kahneman, realizing something else was going on, asked who was happier tearing open that envelope: the person who gained $200,000 or the one who lost $500,000? The obviousness of the answer has a big impact on our decision making. In our minds, losses are more monumental than gains. If we thought only in terms of overall wealth, we'd be more willing to step up to the plate. But that's not how the human brain works.

Oh, and there's one more complicating wrinkle to understand. It's not just a matter of losses being tougher to take than gains. It's a matter of how that loss feels based on where you are standing right now. Imagine for a moment that you are blissfully happy. You are in love. President of a multimillion-dollar company. The most popular person at the country club. And a perfect physical specimen to boot. Got it? Okay, now shift. You don't see any romantic prospects on the horizon. Your job is at a dead-end. And if your pants get any tighter, well, they'll have to pour you into them. Here's the question: You are offered an opportunity to put it all on the line. If you win, you get ten times your wealth. If you lose, you lose everything.

It's a bigger risk to the happier person, so they're less likely to take the bet.

"Many people," says Cornell University Professor Alice Isen, "believe that happy feelings make you impulsive. They make you throw caution to the wind. In fact, they do just the opposite. The happy feelings facilitate self-control, the consideration of how well you'll do long-term, not jumping to conclusions. In this way, happiness is an astonishing resource."

So, as you go through the process of evaluating risks, keep in mind: It's not just a matter of tomorrow, but where you are today. It's not just a matter of how much you stand to win or lose, but how much you stand to win or lose in relation to how much you have and how you feel right now.

Overcoming Our Human Nature

Here's the thing about being human, and it's an important thing to understand as you go about incorporating the principles of The Difference in your life: Once you know how you're likely to behave, you have the power to change what you actually do. Your nature might be to sit on the couch and watch baseball, and yet three times a week like clockwork you turn off the game and go out for a walk or go to the gym. Why? Because your internist or cardiologist told you that regular exercise is part of the recipe for living a longer, healthier life, and you *decided*—yes, there's that word again—to take that advice seriously.

When it comes to risk, the question is "What's the recipe for wealth?" You don't want to take all the risks, just the right ones. You'll see in the examples from our survey, wealthy individuals describe themselves as risk takers far more often than those in any other category . . . even the financially comfortable.

Are you a risk taker?

	Yes
Wealthy	40 percent
Financially comfortable	15 percent
Paycheck-to-paychecks	11 percent
Further-in-debtors	14 percent

Furthermore, for our movers, taking risks was necessary to make the climb.

Attribute	Describes Me	Percent More Likely to Move Forward Than Those Who Said the Word Didn't Describe Them at All
Risk taker	Slightly	1 percent
	Well	5 percent
	Very well	7 percent
	Completely	14 percent

We see that again when we ask about things like entrepreneurship and extreme sports. Taking a risk by starting a business you're passionate about or have a knack for can help you get wealthy, as can investing in the stock market. In fact, it's very difficult to get wealthy without the stock market. (See chapter 11.) But when you hop on a snowboard or decide to make your way to base camp on Mount Everest? Our research shows that although wealthy individuals are more likely to indulge in these pursuits than poorer individuals (perhaps because a guided trek to Everest costs at least $14,000 and requires two weeks off work), these kinds of risks won't make The Difference in your wealth.

Ed Diener, professor of psychology at the University of Illinois, has seen the same in his research. The students he studied who were the highest achievers were willing to take intermediate risks, not crazy risks. They were up for a challenge, certainly, and enjoyed that prospect more than they did a sure thing, but, he recalls, they didn't have the stomach for a million-to-one long shot. "Not every degree of optimism or risk taking is good," he says. "You can have something on your arm that looks kind of blue," he notes. "A moderate risk taker goes to the doctor and gets it checked out. A crazy risk taker blows it off as nothing. In either case it could be melanoma, but only the more moderate person gets the cure."

Survival Is Job One

The wonderful Peter Bernstein, economist, teacher, and author of *Against the Gods: The Remarkable Story of Risk,* has often pointed out something that many other people neglect when thinking about risk, particularly financial risk. "Survival," he has said, "is the only road to riches." In other words, what good is the extra money, power, fame— even love—if you're not around to enjoy the benefits you gain by taking that risk? Whether you'll survive is the first filter you should apply to any risk-reward problem.

The second filter? The risks versus the rewards. What is it you are hoping to accomplish by taking this risk? Will it change your life in the short term? Medium term? Long term? In other words, why are you taking this risk in the first place? If the reward is not meaningful to you, perhaps it's a risk you want to rethink.

The third filter is more complicated. You need to ponder whether or not you can affect the outcome.

The easiest way to think about this is in terms of gambling. You are considering buying a Powerball ticket. The likely outcome is that someone will win a boatload of money and that someone will not be you. I know what they say in the ads: You can't win unless you play. But even if you do play, will that change the outcome? The odds are millions to one against it.

Now think about buying a mutual fund. If you buy into any fund you find, will that improve the likelihood that you will make money? Absolutely not. But what if you did some research on that fund—what if you looked at the three- and five-year returns on that fund, or its Morningstar or Value Line rating? What if you Googled the manager? And what if that research painted a positive picture? Does that improve the chances of your doing well? Absolutely. You are not taking a big risk but, rather, a calculated one. This is a skill that you can learn, a habit that gets better with practice. If you take the time to review the risks you took in the past that did and didn't work out well—and figure out why things unfolded the way they did—you'll learn how to better your odds.

Why Getting Older Is Not Such a Bad Thing, Part II

One more nice thing about getting older is that the risk-reward equation becomes easier to analyze. As we age, we know—as Oprah likes to say, "for sure"—what things mean something to us, and what things don't. And we become more confident in how right we are about those feelings.

Over the past few decades, a study has tracked the confidence of a group of 382 men and women who attended the University of Rochester from the 1960s to the 1980s. It found that two measures of confidence increased as participants moved into middle age. The first was what the researchers called "industry" and described as a feeling of competence. The second they termed "identity" and described as having a solid sense of who you are and what you want out of your life. Both make the risk-filtering process clearer and easier.

Once you pass the three filters, risk taking is a matter of strategy. How do you get yourself to recognize the right risks and then step up to the plate? How do you battle your brain in this process—particularly when you may not know it's putting up a fight? What tactics can you employ? What follows are my favorites.

STRATEGY NUMBER ONE: FORCE A SANITY CHECK

One reason individuals take the wrong risks is that they don't have valid—factual—pictures of the risks they're taking. Case in point: You're adding a deck to the back of your house. You ask your contractor for an estimate and the number he comes back with—$7,500—sounds reasonable. In fact, it sounds more than reasonable. It sounds great. But wait. When was the last time you took on any home improvement project that didn't go over budget? Is your contractor telling you the truth? Or what he needs to tell you to get the job? And once it's well under way, will you start receiving bills for "extras"? That's why getting three estimates is a less risky way to approach the project than settling for just a single estimate. And why those three estimates, supplemented with a report of the average cost of a deck in your part of the country (scaled up or down to the size of your project), is even better. Note: With this strategy, as with many of those on the list, a little push toward reality may be required. Quite often, we don't take the time to get the full picture because we understand it will take us out of fantasyland and into reality. And fantasyland is the more comfortable place to be.

Strategy Number Two: Think Long Term

This is the strategy that drives the most successful investors. It's not about today, tomorrow, next month, or even next year. It's about next decade and the decade after that. This is the window through which you should process all questions about your money or your career: Where do I want to be one year from now, ten years from now, thirty years from now? And does taking this risk move me closer or further away?

This may mean purposefully ignoring the now. Jason Zweig, author of *Your Money and Your Brain: How the New Science of Neuroeconomics Can Help Make You Rich,* has explained to me the concept of "unconscious emotion." Your brain can be reeling from very powerful feelings and yet you, the person, can be on tape-delay. You may not understand what is happening in that brain of yours. And that can drive you to act irrationally, taking risks you shouldn't take instead of the risks you should.

Let's say you're opening the mail and come to your quarterly 401(k) statement. You rip open the envelope and . . . and . . . it's a beautiful specimen. You trounced the market and, even though you might not be conscious of it, there's a decent chance your brain thinks you're an investing genius on par with, say, Warren Buffett. If you happen to turn on CNBC precisely at that moment, you might believe in your own prowess so much that you make an abnormally large bet on the stock being discussed on the screen. No matter that the stock doesn't fit into your asset allocation. No matter that you don't buy individual stocks, only mutual funds. You've experienced a big gain and the rush that goes along with it, and you're going to be tempted to try to replicate that feeling—not only today, but whenever you evaluate a financial opportunity in the future.

This is precisely where a long-term outlook—and plan—are necessary. They give you parameters in which you are allowed to take risks. If that stock happens to fill up an asset allocation bucket that you'd previously set (if this is an international play, for instance, and right now you're low on that), if you did your homework and understood the case for that stock, well that's one story. But if it's an outlier, your long-term plan is a good reason to tell yourself no.

STRATEGY NUMBER THREE: UNDERSTAND YOUR LIZARD BRAIN

I wasn't the first person to say it and I certainly won't be the last: Men take more risks than women, in money and in life. You can blame our lizard brains for that. Men, the traditional hunters, had to go out and put their lives on the line to slay dragons (or more likely buffalo or bison), or they—and everyone who depended on them—would starve to death. The kill brought on a good old-fashioned adrenaline rush. Women, the traditional gatherers, stayed back to protect the young. To this day, taking a risk feels more pleasurable and less (for lack of a better word) risky to a man than it does to a woman.

Sometimes you need to think outside that traditional comfort zone. As a man, you need to understand: Am I doing this because I need the high that comes with taking this risk? Would running a few miles give me the same satisfaction? As a woman: Am I not doing this simply because it feels foreign or "not like me"? For women in particular, a very important follow-up question is: "What happens if I don't do it?" What is the risk of *not* taking this job, *not* buying this investment, *not* meeting this person? We often forget that there is often as much risk in *not* acting as there is in putting yourself on the line.

STRATEGY NUMBER FOUR: WHEN ALL ELSE FAILS, RUN!

Brett N. Steenbarger, a clinical psychologist and author of *Enhancing Trader Performance: Proven Strategies from the Cutting Edge of Trading Psychology,* explains that when we humans experience a powerful emotional event (and a big gain or loss in our wealth is one, even if it's just on paper), our brains don't work the way they do when we're calm. During times like these, the analytical part of the brain shuts down, Steenbarger explains.

Again, this is where you need that plan, those goals—for your investments, your business, your life—to keep yourself on the straight and narrow even when your brain fails you.

In the heat of the moment, you may also want to consider fleeing the scene. If you feel like you're about to make a bad decision, go to the movies. Go out to dinner. Or, as I do, go on a run. Immerse yourself in a twelve-hour *Law and Order* marathon. Or cook your way through the veggies section of your favorite recipe book. In other words: Stop paying so much attention to the daily movements in your portfolio and focus a little more on your life.

Why You Should Listen to Your Gut

A short story: Years ago I was recruited to be a writer for the just-about-to-launch *SmartMoney* magazine. There were, according to my legal pad analysis, as many reasons not to take the job as there were to take it. My current job at *Forbes* provided stability; *SmartMoney* was a start-up. I was doing well at *Forbes;* I'd have to prove myself at *Smart-Money*. When I was working on a story for *Forbes* and called a source, they would immediately come to the phone; a call from *SmartMoney* was likely to elicit a "Huh?" The *Forbes* job had been hard to get and this seemed, by comparison, too easy. And so on. And yet . . . something told me to go. It wasn't the money. It wasn't the promotion. I couldn't put my finger on it—which meant I couldn't explain it to my parents or my husband, which meant that they thought I should stay where I was.

It was my gut. My intuition. My sixth sense. Call it what you want, but against all advice I went to *SmartMoney*. It was the best career move I ever made. And there have been other situations like it. Most decisions that I have had that very strong feeling about have—in the end—been good decisions. And research says that's the way it is for most people. Especially people who know The Difference.

Can you easily read other people?	
Wealthy	42%
Financially Comfortable	27%
Paycheck-to-paychecks	25%
Further-in-debtors	30%

It's Called Intuition—and Men Have It, Too

What, exactly, is intuition? What's the scientific definition? Psychology professor Dave Myers of Hope College in Michigan describes it this way: Intuition is a learned expertise that's instantly accessible.

That makes sense. Consider a basic task like driving. It initially requires great concentration. With practice, it becomes automatic. Your hands and feet do it intuitively while your mind can be elsewhere. For some, more complicated tasks operate from intuition as well. Chess masters, Myers says, can look at a board and intuitively know the right move.

That's because intuition doesn't appear out of thin air. Our brains are computers that, over the years, have stored up scads of patterns. We have gathered information that tells us if one thing happens, something else is likely to follow. This information is felt in our gut.

Some problems are better suited to being solved intuitively than others. Intuition is helpful at reading emotions in other people's faces. It's not great for picking stocks or predicting the outcome of the big game, though.

It's also true that some people are more intuitive than others (and some people—our further-in-debtors—think they are more intuitive than they actually are). But you can—and should—learn this skill if you aspire to wealth.

You first must make some room for your intuition. If you are focusing all your energies on solving a particular problem, there is little room in your brain for your intuition to marinate with it. Sometimes you just have to relax and clear the air. I've often noticed I have those "aha" moments not when I'm searching for them, but when I abandon the dilemma and go for a run or take a shower. That's when the light goes on. And I'm not the only one.

Psychologist Dave Myers shared the story of Andrew Wiles, the solver of a centuries-old mathematical problem, "Fermat's last theorem." Wiles noted that the task required not just effort but relaxation. "You have to really think about nothing but that problem—just concentrate on it. Then you stop. Afterwards there seems to be a kind of period of relaxation during which the subconscious appears to take over, and it's during that time that some new insight comes."

What else can you do to use your intuition to your best advantage?

HARNESS IT. What if you can't access your gut feelings? It happens. You really aren't sure if you're feeling one way or the other. Flip a coin. Decide one outcome is heads, the other is tails. When the coin is in the air, pay attention. You will hope it will land one way or the other. That hope is intuition.

SCRUTINIZE IT. Once you know what your intuition is saying, the next question to ask yourself is "Will it work in this situation?" Take what your intuition is telling you and imagine carrying it out. See if you notice any warning signs or red flags. Those signs, those flags, are your intuition talking. Use them to continue along your path—or to change it.

CONDUCT A "PRE-MORTEM." Take both alternatives. Imagine each has gone badly six months down the road and ask yourself which makes you feel worse. When you run a scenario that way and start realizing all of the ways that you can get into trouble, very often you'll appreciate what you're up against. This sort of forecasting, while not always present, can make a decision a little clearer.

DO A REAL POSTMORTEM. Once you've used your intuition to guide you through a challenge, take note of how well it served you—or didn't serve you. Essentially you're making a conscious choice to learn from your experience. Note not only that it did or didn't work out, but why. Maybe you can do it differently the next time.

As you start using your intuition, you'll start to trust it more. That's a good thing—until it's not. Moderation, in this as in so many elements of The Difference, is the key. If your intuition drives you too close to the edge—and your success makes you arrogant—you could fail. That's why the pre-mortem is important, especially for successful individuals. Close to the edge is a good thing. Over it—not so much.

Making Your Own Luck

I should point out that luck doesn't seem to be a factor in The Difference. People who've moved out of a quadrant in which they're struggling financially don't credit good luck with their rise. Those who've slid backward don't blame bad luck for their fall.

So why discuss it? Because research has shown that feeling lucky can help you attain other attributes that *are* important parts of the equation. Feeling that the cards may fall your way can open you to possibilities; can make you present a more positive, optimistic face; and can make you more attractive to others, which makes it likelier that they will connect with you (very important, as you'll see in the next chapter)—even though you don't realize precisely what is going on. (It's also hard to pinpoint the exact spot where smart risk taking or intuition end and luck takes over.)

The credit for much of this research goes to Richard Wiseman, a psychologist and researcher at the University of Hertfordshire in England and author of *The Luck Factor: Change Your Luck, Change Your Life.* You can improve your own odds in the lottery of life, Wiseman's research says, by understanding there's a big difference between chance and luck. A game of chance is one in which there is no control. People don't win time and time again. Luck is something we create by turning the risks of various events in our favor. We try new things. We look out for new opportunities. We are ready to receive the unexpected.

Wiseman and his colleagues learned this by conducting an experiment asking subjects to turn pages of a newspaper and count the photos. A few pages in, adjacent to a photo so it would be hard to miss, was a big advertisement that said STOP COUNTING. THERE ARE 43 PHOTOGRAPHS IN THIS NEWSPAPER. A few pages later, there was another ad that said STOP COUNTING: TELL THE EXPERIMENTER YOU'VE SEEN THIS AND WIN 150 POUNDS. Unlucky people—or rather people who claimed to be unlucky—tended not to notice either one. Those who considered themselves lucky noticed both. They'd give the answer—forty-three—then ask if they should proceed, then a few minutes later, break into a big smile and ask if they were really getting the money. These lucky folks were open to the fact that perhaps there was more to the exercise than the experimenter described. The unlucky kept their eyes on one specific goal and missed everything else around them.

Fortunately, like other elements in this book, luck can be taught. Wiseman himself runs a program called Luck School. But there's much you can do on your own without going back to school.

YOU CAN LOOK FOR THE GOOD IN EVERYTHING. Lucky people find the silver lining. Yes, it poured on your wedding day, and you had to hold the ceremony outside because you hadn't planned an alternative. And you got mud on your dress. But the canopy formed by the guests' umbrellas fostered a sense of intimacy you wouldn't have experienced otherwise. The light from the cloudy sky made everyone look beautiful in the photos. It smelled like spring. And no one will ever, ever forget that wedding.

YOU CAN SAY "YES" RATHER THAN "NO." This, in and of itself, puts you in the path of people and opportunities. The writer Patricia Volk penned an essay in *O, the Oprah Magazine* about her year of saying "yes." A traditional nay-saying, sit-at-home, stick-her-nose-in-a-book kind of person, she decided that for one year she would completely change her ways. What followed? A blind date with a famous person and a day of outlet shopping with one of only two fashion icons ever chosen to have a retrospective of her clothing in the Metropolitan Museum of Art.

YOU CAN NOTICE THE GOOD—LUCKY—THINGS THAT ARE ALREADY HAPPENING IN YOUR LIFE. Say to yourself: "That's a good thing." Simultaneously, make yourself not log the unlucky things. Your mind will take note of the fact that this is a new pattern—a pattern of luck and good fortune.

Exercise: The Risk Filter

Fear is an emotion, just like stress, anxiety, and worry are emotions. They manifest themselves in different ways in different people. Fear may set your heart racing, anxiety your stomach churning. Worry may keep you up at night. Risk is different. It's a calculation. And all of these emotions play a role in working the variables of this calculation as correctly as possible.

One of the most important things to know as you approach any risk—financial or otherwise—is that it is normal to be anxious. It is normal to have fear. In fact, people who don't have it—elite athletes, for example, who don't get the willies before a big meet or game—perform less well than those who feel some stress about what's coming.

According to research done by the Connecticut-based Harrison Group, 65 percent of wealthy individuals have a disquieting anxiety that the wheels could come off the bus at any time and that their assets will not sustain them. In part, that is due to the circles they run in. Most know someone who got blown up in a merger, an acquisition, a start-up, or a spin-off.

But for these people, the fear is overcome by a sense of having to do something—sometimes by a sense of duty, other times by a sense of knowing that if you don't do it, you will deeply regret it down the road.

That's why I suggest this exercise. It involves asking yourself two filtering questions as you approach any risk.

"What happens to me if I do this?"
and
"What happens to me if I don't?"

The risk of inaction should always be pondered, yet all too often, it's forgotten. And in many cases, these two questions will point you in precisely the right direction.

Exercise: Reframe Your Risks

Which sounds better to you: an investment or risk that has an 80 percent chance of success, or an investment or risk that has a 20 percent chance of failure? If you're like most people, the former does. And yet, particularly to those of us who tend to be pessimists (if you don't know where you stand, take the test in chapter 5), the second scenario is the natural default.

If you're used to thinking this way, it's important to understand that it's as much nurture as nature. You can train yourself to do the opposite. It's just a matter of making a conscious choice to do so.

SCENARIO: You're headed to a dinner party given by one of your friends for a crowd from her office. You're nervous because you'll know only one person in the room.

OLD THOUGHT: I am going to have a miserable time and probably dribble guacamole on my shirt.

NEW THOUGHT: Maybe I'll meet someone to play tennis with this weekend.

SCENARIO: Your boss just announced she's going to retire at fifty. You want the job but you're pretty sure the guy in the next office does also.

OLD THOUGHT: He's been there longer than I have. I don't have a shot.

NEW THOUGHT: My last three months have been stellar. I improved productivity on the eastern route and saved the company $3 million. I am going to make sure they know that I want to be considered, and if they don't give me this job, at least they'll know I'm ready for what comes along next.

SCENARIO: You have an idea for a new venture. Taking the plunge means quitting your job and relying on yourself for the next twelve months.

OLD THOUGHT: What makes me think my idea is better than the six hundred that fail every single day? I'm safer here with a paycheck and benefits.

NEW THOUGHT: I have thoroughly researched this market and there's nothing out there like my product. There's a need. And I have enough money set aside to do it without sabotaging my family or my retirement.

Remember: If you don't ask, the answer will always be no. If you don't try, you will never succeed. And, as my rabbi friends like to say, if not now—when?

A Quick Guide to Chapter 8

We've all seen people move up the rungs of success from time to time and whispered (sometimes less than kindly), "Connections." They're not imagined, and they're proven to work. People with the right kind of links to others at work, from college, in the neighborhood, or through some sort of professional organization, can—if they know what they're doing—use those links to get noticed, get promotions, and get raises, all faster than would have happened if they were going it alone. In this chapter, you'll find an exercise for breaking out of your shell, learn how to navigate the Internet to make the right kind of allegiances, and meet a guy whose church family turned into his very best source of customers.

MEET HARRY

AGE: Forty-eight
FAMILY: Married, two kids
ASSETS: $1 million to $2.5 million
HARRY'S DIFFERENCES: Hardworking, connected, takes risks, resilient, intuitive

There are people who make time for the other people in their lives— and there are people who don't. Harry is one of the former. He prioritizes the connections he has with his community, whether it's his church community, his wife and children, or the people he works with. And as he explains, those priorities have been at the heart of his success.

Q: *What's the secret to your success?*
A: I worked hard for twenty years, bought real estate, and stayed away from the stock market. I learned the hard way that stocks are a sucker bet.

Q: Your user name is "modemguy." Why did you choose that?

A: One of my many sidelines is working as a Time Warner cable installer. I've got no formal technical training. My dad started a computer business in 1982. He worked in computer standards for the government but took a buyout during the Reagan era. I started working for him in '83 and I bought him out in '87.

Q: What kind of business was it?

A: It was a church ministry automation business. Doing church computer work in the 1980s. It grew out of his volunteer position as head of the finance committee for a Baptist church.

Q: Is church an important part of your life?

A: Yes, I met my wife at a Baptist church where I was doing an installation. I have many friends from church—and a lot of business contacts, too. Now we go to a Gospel Church in South Carolina.

Q: How did the church automation software business work?

A: We offered a menu of choices. If the church didn't want payroll or a full accounting package, they could buy the membership module, which was strictly a database of names and addresses, and/or the contribution module, which kept track of what people donated. We got lucky when the Mormon, Church of Latter-Day Saints, bought the package for contributions for many of their D.C. churches.

Q: You sound pretty techy.

A: I'm a programmer, but I've always been in business for myself. I started a fence company at age seventeen and sold it at age twenty-one. As a kid, I was always cutting grass, delivering newspapers, cutting firewood.

My grandparents influenced me a lot. My grandfather was a pharmacist and my grandmother had rental properties and sold peaches in her front yard. They were Depression-era people who did what it took to make ends meet. They were just high school graduates. My dad was the first in the family to go to college.

Q: What's your educational background?
A: I had a double major in agriculture and accounting.

Q: Let's go back to the company you and your dad had. Tell me about the history of that.
A: In 1987, our family exploded over control of the company. I'm an only child. And it was my mother and me against my father. I bought my father out and got control of company. My parents separated, but they eventually got back together. By 1989, I had back-to-back years of $1.2 million in sales, and I booked $400,000 net profits. I needed more space for my employees. Right off the bat, I decided not to rent space but to buy. I bought a couple of townhouses, paid them off, and never looked back. My wife and I now have fourteen properties in North Carolina.

Q: So are you in real estate full-time or are you still in the tech business?
A: I'm retired, but I'm installing phones, networks, and wireless for a time-share guy.

Q: Retired? You're forty-eight years old.
A: Well, 9/11 was a big factor in my decision. We had a contract to do computer work at the Pentagon. Our customers were in a trailer and blown off their feet when the American Airlines plane hit the Pentagon. That made me think long and hard, and it resulted in some big changes. Real estate went through the roof in 2004. We decided to sell our properties and move to Myrtle Beach. The market was insane at the time. We put our houses on the market and got buyers within two weeks.

Q: Clearly, you've followed your own path.

A: I broke the rule that says you have to get a job with a Fortune 1000 company, work nine to five, and join the rat race. There have been plenty of days when I've worked twelve to fifteen hours a day, but all the money was going in my pocket. I also have a healthy spiritual life and I take care of myself physically. I set time aside for God and for hitting golf balls and time for my wife. People get divorced because they work all the time and don't make time for each other.

Q: It's interesting because even though you've been very successful, you're not a classic workaholic who is running himself into the ground.

A: Well, I had a career goal to make my first million by thirty-five. Did it by forty-five.

Q: Where did that ambition come from?

A: My first class at Ohio State was an economics class. The professor changed my life. He explained about the opportunity cost of the four years we were spending in college. He told us before you get married, get the nice house, the nice car. Try a goldfish, a house plant, and some pets before you have kids. Learn how to love something other than yourself.

He said there was research that proved that the longer you waited to get married and have a family, the more money you would end up with. My wife and I got married at thirty-three. By that time I had a Porsche and a delivery van for the computers. She was a schoolteacher. We had three kids before age forty-one.

Q: Besides finding a wife, have you met people at church who have helped you in business?

A: Yes, there are a lot of trade associations in my area, and I started getting trade association work from people I knew at church. They said, "If Harry can do computers, he can do phone systems." Then I started doing phone work for doctors, churches. The more you do for people, the more they want you to do. All of a sudden, I'm wearing three or four hats.

CHAPTER EIGHT

The Kevin Bacon Principle

You may at some time in your life played the six degrees game, where you sit down and try—with six connections or fewer—to connect the star of *Footloose* and *Diner* to some other famous person, or yourself to someone, famous or not. Six degrees is loosely derived from the Do You Know (fill in the blank) conversations played among people who went to the same college, grew up in the same town, joined the same fraternity, or worked—at one time—for the same company. States and cities have their own versions. (Texas Exes, anyone?) Jewish Geography is another offshoot.

This may seem like fun and games. But, in fact, these social connections play a role in success and wealth. One 1988 study of managers found that the most successful ones spent 70 percent more time networking and 10 percent more time in routine communication (back then, this meant talking on the phone) than their less successful counterparts. Our study asked questions regarding social connections a number of ways.

How satisfied do you feel with your social life?

	Very Satisfied
Wealthy	46 percent
Financially comfortable	38 percent
Paycheck-to-paychecks	24 percent
Further-in-debtors	13 percent

How satisfied do you feel with your community?

	Very Satisfied
Wealthy	40 percent
Financially comfortable	33 percent
Paycheck-to-paychecks	21 percent
Further-in-debtors	11 percent

Would you say you're popular?

	Yes
Wealthy	45 percent
Financially comfortable	24 percent
Paycheck-to-paychecks	17 percent
Further-in-debtors	17 percent

Interestingly, the range of people with whom the wealthy and financially comfortable socialize is much wider than average. Paycheck-to-paychecks and further-in-debtors are more likely to stick to their families; those doing better certainly spend time with their families but also enjoy the company of others who share their interests—neighbors, coworkers, and people who could help them advance financially or in their careers.

For the movers in our survey—those who jumped from the bottom two groups to the top two—outgoing personality traits made a significant difference. Those who said the word "popular" described them well or very well were 20 and 22 percent more likely to make the leap, respectively, than those who said it did not describe them at all.

How Connected Are You?

So here's the question: Do you have enough people in your circle? Do you have the support that you need to get ahead?

Researcher Charles S. Carver developed a number of helpful diagnostic tools over the course of his career. One was the optimism test you took in chapter 5. The test that follows is based on another in his arsenal. It was originally created to determine if the amount of support a breast cancer patient receives changes her life for the better. It showed that yes, more support leads to better well-being—and a better sex life.

It turns out that having a network of support in your life leads to a better prognosis for wealth as well.

Here's how to take this test: Think back to the last time you had a real problem. It could be something you faced at work or a problem you dealt with at home. Then answer the following questions on a scale of 0 to 4, with 0 being "Not at all" and 4 being "Completely."

1. How much did the primary person / most important people in your life give you advice or information about the problem (whether you wanted it or not)?

2. How much did that person / those people help you with things related to your problem (for example, taking other items off your plate so you could focus or helping you find the right sources of information or additional support)?

3. How much did that person / those people give you reassurance, encouragement, and emotional support (affection) concerning your problem?

4. How much did that person / those people listen to and try to understand your worries about your problem?

5. How much can you relax and be yourself around that person / those people?

6. How much can you open up to that person / those people if you need to talk about your worries about the problem?

7. How often does that person / those people argue with you relating to your problem?

8. How often does that person / those people criticize you relating to your problem?

9. How often does that person / those people let you down when you are counting on him / her / them?

10. How often does that person / those people withdraw from discussions about your problem or try to change the topic away from your problem?

Scoring: Score questions 1 through 6 according to the 4 scale. Score questions 7 through 10 in reverse: 4=0; 3=1; 2=2; 1=3; 0=4. Then add up the numbers.

The highest score is 40 out of 40. If you scored 30 or above, you have a decent amount of support in your life. From 20 to 30, you have a moderate amount but feel like more would be beneficial. If you scored below 20, this is an area where you could use some work.

I know that sounds strange, to say *you* need work. After all, we are looking at the behaviors of others—behaviors that are not under your control. But the truth is, those other people are reacting to the energy, feelings, and effort you put out to them. By altering your own behaviors, you can influence what comes back to you. You can drive whether people have a positive or negative experience when in your presence. And that makes all the difference in the world.

Why It Pays to Be Connected

Ever heard of "social capital"? This is the currency of connections. Social capital is the asset that is created when relationships between people change in ways that lead to action, generally for the good. Joe introduces you to Judy, who is so taken by your funny-yet-insightful banter that she immediately thinks of you when her company is looking to hire a consultant in your field. That's social capital at work.

Like stocks, real estate, or other assets, social capital has value—sometimes huge value. But you may not be able to measure it in dollars and cents. Its currencies are information, resources, and sponsorship (when someone puts his or her neck out to further your career or help you in some other way). Social capital can net you promotions, jumps in salary, helpful contacts for the future, and—often just as important—satisfaction.

Interestingly, researchers have found that a person doesn't have to be your best friend for that connection to provide a significant payoff. Surprisingly, weak ties in the workforce can be more valuable than strong ones. If you have a close relationship with someone that is emotionally intense with frequent interactions, it may operate on more than one platform—that is, you might be friends as well as coworkers. These are the people with whom you are likely to share your secrets or fears.

A weak tie is formed when you are both connected to a third person—a friend of a friend—or connected to a common network, such as an alumni association. You have less frequent contact with this person, or those contacts are more superficial in nature, yet these weak ties have been shown to be the most important source of information on jobs. And they can help in boosting your salary, getting you a promotion, increasing your career satisfaction, and gaining access to information. The more of these weak ties you have, the better. So invest in casting a wide, but careful, net.

Research by Dr. Robert Liden, an expert in organizational behavior at the University of Illinois at Chicago, has shown that increasing your visibility within your company can lead to more promotions and higher compensation. Being visible means connecting with people in your organization who are outside your own function or area, preferably at a higher pay grade. If you know people at higher levels, you may be able to access equipment or support you need to do your job better. You may learn about training programs you wouldn't know about otherwise. You may discover information—and therefore opportunities—in the company that other people in your small unit might not be aware of, which gives you an advantage over them. You may even find a mentor.

Other pursuits worth the effort: Joining professional organizations. Getting involved in community activities. And saying "yes" to those drinks after work.

Of course, being choosy about the people with whom you socialize—on the job or off—is important. Liden and his colleagues conducted a separate study that showed while connections to people who are well thought of can help you, close ties to people who are not well respected can diminish your reputation. In other words, your mother was right. You are judged by the company you keep.

Lucky Breaks? Maybe Not

If you're not yet convinced that connecting is a good thing, here's one more piece of evidence: Connections are closely linked to luck (which, as we talked about in the last chapter, is linked to success, which is linked to wealth . . . you know how this works by now, don't you?). Luck researcher Richard Wiseman conducted an experiment in which he asked people first to tell him whether they were lucky, unlucky, or neither. Then he handed them a list of fifteen last names common in the United Kingdom and asked people to indicate if they were on a first-name basis with at least one person with each last name. Nearly half of the lucky people had eight or more last names on their list, compared with one-quarter of the unlucky and one-third of the neithers.

Why was it that the self-described "lucky" folks had more connections? Why did they know more people with last names on that list? Because they were open to not only new experiences but new acquaintances who may at some point turn into contacts, mentors, or friends.

For a shy person or someone who hasn't been successful at connecting in the past, meeting someone can be a painful experience. But knowing that scientists believe that we live in a world where just about any other person—not just fans of Kevin Bacon games—is a scant six links away may bolster your confidence to stick your neck out. Wiseman is not the only researcher to test the theory. Back in the 1960s, psychologist Stanley Milgram sent letters to three hundred randomly selected people in Nebraska and Kansas and asked them to help that letter make its way to a target person—a particular stockbroker in Boston, Massachusetts. Rather than sending the letter to the stockbroker, however, participants were instructed to send their letter to someone they knew on a first-name basis who they thought might know the stockbroker. The person who received that letter was asked to do the same.

The results: Three decades before the Internet and four before Facebook, nearly one-third of the letters actually made it to their destination. And on average, each of those letters made just five stops—it took six people to make the connection between the first randomly selected Kansan or Nebraskan and the Boston stockbroker. So take the plunge.

But What If You're Not an Extrovert?

Woody Allen was only partially correct when he said 80 percent of success was showing up. You not only have to be there—you have to be there and then you have to get involved with people. "What you need to do is allow people to see that you're competent, as well as nice and a good person," explains Monica Forret, professor of business at St. Ambrose University, who started studying networking after noting that some people are really good at it, while others are not. People who were raised in higher socioeconomic households tend to have an edge, she says, not necessarily because they're more outgoing, but because they've seen this sort of behavior all their lives. If your parents know people in positions of power, then chances are you do as well. The introductions have been made. But even if you haven't got those chits in your back pocket, this is a skill you can learn. "You can be strategic about this," she says.

How?

USE, BUT DON'T OVERUSE, TECHNOLOGY. In some ways, technology is networking's savior. You don't have to constantly update and erase your address book, it's more of a living organism. And there are so many ways for you to reach out and touch friends, colleagues, and contacts through the year that aren't at all cumbersome. But all tools—from Facebook and LinkedIn to your BlackBerry or cell phone—are only as good as the person behind them. Having a MySpace page isn't going to do anything for you unless you tell people it's there and then use it to stay in touch with people.

IT'S NOT TRANSACTIONAL, IT'S RELATIONAL. Networking expert Diane Darling shared this piece of advice with me: The biggest mistake busy people make is to allow themselves to lose touch with others. They lose themselves in the work and then the work ends and they need something: a contact, a position, a favor. But if you haven't been in touch recently, picking up the phone just to ask for something can be very tough. (If you do have to do this, call and say you're sorry you've been AWOL, but their name came to mind because you're looking for a job in the field. If it's the first time you've dropped the ball with this person, chances are you'll be forgiven. The second or third? Perhaps not.) It's also a reason to do favors "just because." If someone asks you for a favor, in business or in life, and you have the ability to do it without its taking a huge toll on your family or your own work, do it. It'll come right back to you.

ASK YOURSELF, WHY AM I DOING THIS? There are all types of connections. Before you start joining every club in school (the Jan Brady approach, for children of the 1970s), think about what you're trying to accomplish. If you want to build a consulting business, perhaps you want to join a service organization that has a lot of business professionals in it. If you're looking to raise funds for a start-up, perhaps the alumni group of your college or university would be more appropriate. And if you're looking to work your way up the corporate ladder, maybe you should join something social at work—the AIDS or breast cancer walk team, for example—to let people see you in another light.

UNDERSTAND THAT JOINING ISN'T ENOUGH. If you show up but don't actually get your hands dirty, you're not accomplishing anything. You need to find your way into a leadership role. That means figuring out which committees are the most meaningful and valued and then volunteering for them. It may mean finding one person you can talk to and asking them to nominate you to serve on the board. You have to build trust with other people before you can actually use this network you're building.

GIVE A LITTLE TO GET A LITTLE. The goal of connecting, Forret points out, is becoming someone that others are willing to help. The best way to get someone to help you is to do something to help them first. That doesn't mean getting their child a job for the summer or finagling them an impossible-to-get invitation to an exclusive party. Those are things only the already-connected can offer. But how about offering a lift to the office after you hear their car is in the shop? How about taking some responsibilities off their shoulders after learning that this is a particularly tough week at work? People who network ineffectively are under the mistaken impression that it's all about them. It's not—it's all about the person on the other side of the equation. After their needs are satisfied, you can ask for help or, better yet, advice.

THE DOCTOR IS IN. Yes, advice. When you're looking to strengthen a relatively new connection, asking for advice is preferable to asking for help for two reasons. First, it's flattering. When you ask someone for advice, you're showing them you value their knowledge.

Tell them you see they've had this incredible career or success and you'd like to know more about it. Second, advice doesn't require the person you're connecting with to ask anything of someone else. It's easier to offer and doesn't require the expenditure of any of that person's social capital. That means, particularly if you're a new acquaintance, it's a smaller risk, and for that reason alone you're more likely to get what you're asking for. Don't be surprised if in the course of conversation the person offers help as well.

FOLLOW UP. If someone offers you help, take them up on it. Say a new connection offers to introduce you to Fred, his next-door neighbor, who just happens to hire people with your skills. The fact that they made the offer does not mean that they're going to chase you down and schedule that meeting. The very next day, place a call or send an e-mail expressing your gratitude and asking for the phone number so you can follow up yourself. That will ensure that your new connection does as promised and, by rounding back so quickly, you're signaling how much you value his or her help or advice.

SAY "THANK YOU." The next chapter is all about the link between gratitude and success, but it deserves a mention here. At the risk of sounding like your mother, when someone helps you network, you need to say "Thank you." Better yet, write an actual thank-you note— not a thank-you e-mail, not a thank-you phone call, a thank-you *note*. On paper. I know, you're busy. But let me just say that over the course of my career, I have interviewed many people much busier than you or me. And it's been striking to me how the very busiest—and, yes, most successful—of those people have been the ones to drop me handwritten notes. I have saved notes from Jack Welch, Richard Holbrooke, and Jamie Lee Curtis, among others, and as a result I try to be sure every guest on my radio show gets one as well.

HABITS THAT HELP / HABITS THAT HURT:
HAVING CHILDREN

When it comes to families and wealth, is the smallest the best? You'd think it might be. Fewer mouths to feed means more money in the bank. That would make singles the wealthiest people on the planet. In fact, it doesn't work that way. Marriage, as you read earlier, is linked to wealth. And children—if not already in the picture, knowing they may be on the way soon—give adults that kick in the pants they didn't have in their single days to start putting money away and investing it for the future.

The cheaper-by-the-dozen phenomenon, though, turns out to be better on the big screen than in real life. One child, explains researcher Lisa Keister, inspires you to start saving more. Two or three, however, make it more difficult to save. There are not only more individuals to put food on the table for each night, there are soccer dues, choir uniforms, summer camp, and eventually—yikes—college tuition bills. Buying a family home makes stashing away the big bucks even more difficult. (That's one reason that it's so important to pay down the mortgage, rather than use it as a piggy bank. Your mortgage, if you're using it to build equity rather than simply pay for the place in which you're living, is another form of forced savings. In a good scenario, the home is paid off by the time you retire. Then you can trade down and use the money to bolster your nest egg. In a great scenario, the home is paid off by the time the kids go off to college. At that point, if home equity debt is cheaper than student loans, you have another source of capital at your disposal.)

So what is the best thing to do in this situation?

When you add to the family, don't immediately increase your spending. Do you *need* a bigger home? Not necessarily. There was a time when children routinely shared bedrooms. Some still think it's fun. Do you *need* a bigger, newer car? Again, not necessarily. When we make these purchases without considering what other costs are coming our way, we can get caught in a cash squeeze. And, if you're planning to shift from being a two-income family to a one-income family, use pregnancy to road test the process. For nine months (or however long it is after you realize the stick is blue), live on one income and bank the other. This gives you the security of knowing that (a) you can do it, and (b) you've got a solid chunk of cash in reserve for emergencies. Finally, there's divorce. In some cases it's unavoidable—but you should know that Zagorsky's work shows it is the fastest way to destroy your wealth.

Why It's Good to Feel Good About Yourself

One big barrier to connecting with others is harboring negative views about yourself. Our study showed that a hefty helping of self-esteem and confidence is closely tied to wealth.

Would you say the word "confident" describes you very well?	
	Yes
Wealthy	63 percent
Financially comfortable	54 percent
Paycheck-to-paychecks	40 percent
Further-in-debtors	33 percent

Likewise, it boosted our movers out of their financially troubled zones and into prosperity.

Attribute	Describes Me	Percent More Likely to Move Forward Than Those Who Said the Word Didn't Describe Them at All
Confident	Slightly	16 percent
	Well	34 percent
	Very well	33 percent
	Completely	28 percent

Again, these findings have plenty of backup. Feeling positive about your self-worth, your competence, and the amount of control you have over your life predicts a higher income—and therefore greater wealth, says Timothy Judge, management professor at the University of Florida. And, he notes, virtually everyone has some sort of narrative running through their mind about their general competence level. In other words, people who feel they are generally competent at work tend to feel the same at home, in social situations, and so on.

Although it is difficult to change your concept of yourself, it is helpful to understand it, so that you can turn it into a positive. For example, Judge says that he is very self-critical. Rather than spending time trying to change himself or convince himself that he's okay, he focuses on recognizing the benefits of this trait. "If I keep telling myself how wonderful I am, I start to ossify and stop learning," he says.

Fake It Till You Make It, Part II

By the time this book is published, I will have been speaking to large groups of people for more than a decade. When I first started doing this, I got nervous each and every time. These days, I get nervous selectively. But I remember the worst case of nerves I ever had: I was hired to speak to something called the Economics Club of . . . I don't remember where it was, but it was a midsize city somewhere in the middle of the country—perhaps Cleveland or Des Moines. And I was petrified. Why? Because of the title of the organization. I had spoken to plenty of university groups, plenty of Junior Leagues, my share of Jewish Federations, a decent number of corporate getaways, even the occasional medical or dental convention. But an "Economics Club," in my mind, was going to be filled with Ben Stein clones and wannabes. These people were, no doubt, going to fall asleep halfway through my talk on money and happiness. I would, no doubt, fall apart during Q&A.

I thought about canceling, but the contract had been signed and the paycheck was a nice one. So I decided I would get my energy way up, go in there with a smile on my face, and radiate confidence. And then I started by telling them precisely what I was not: not an economist, not an MBA, not a financial planner. And what I was and am: a journalist who has spent the last fifteen years immersed in the world of other people's money.

I was—it turned out—petrified for nothing. This Economics Club, like many around the country I later learned, was essentially another name for members of the chamber of commerce. It was an audience full of smart people, absolutely, but these smart people hadn't heard my "Money and Happiness" talk before, and they hung on every word. And then they asked me questions that—by and large—I could answer.

And when I could not answer—for this talk and every other since—I stand by my one rule: I don't bullshit. I confidently explain that I do not know the answer and that to give them one off the top of my head would be a grave disservice, particularly in this economy. Then I always try to provide a suggestion of where the right answer might be found. And you know what? When you say it like that, "I don't know" is perfectly acceptable.

Exercise: Get in Touch with Your Inner Values and Boost Your Self-esteem

Research has shown that writing about values that are personally important to you can help you look at the world outwardly, rather than inwardly. In one experiment, conducted by the University of Michigan psychologist Jennifer Crocker and her colleagues, students were asked to rank the following values in order of importance: business, art / music / theater, social life / relationships, science / pursuit of knowledge, religion / morality, government / politics. Then they were handed an envelope that asked them either to spend ten minutes writing about the value that was most important to them or ten minutes writing about the value that was least important to them (including an explanation of why it might be meaningful to other people). Those students who were asked to write about their most important value then rated "how much they felt" eighteen feelings, including love, connectedness, empathy, pride, power, weakness, and defensiveness. No matter which value the students chose as most important, writing about it increased their feelings of love and connectedness—and decreased feelings of defensiveness. In other words, it provided a self-esteem boost that made these students more immune to the pressures of the outside world.

Why does this work? Crocker and her colleagues believe the writing exercise helps you escape your boundaries by reminding you what you care about, other than yourself. Furthermore, feeling loved and connected may also dampen your defenses so that you can absorb useful-but-threatening information, such as on-the-job criticism or a spouse's nudge to do something differently.

Now you try it: Take ten minutes and write about the value that is most important to you. First, choose one from this list: business, art / music / theater, social life / relationships, science / pursuit of knowledge, religion / morality, government / politics.

Ask yourself why it is important to you. What about it do you value? A week later, do the exercise again. Then try to notice if you feel calmer on the days you do the writing. Do you feel less agitated? Safer? More secure? If so, it's working. If this is an exercise you don't have time for on a regular basis, Crocker suggests using it before you face, say, your next performance review. It's helpful in any difficult situation or when you find yourself losing track of what's really important.

A Quick Guide to Chapter 9

Americans blew it in the translation. When the Spanish or the Italians say "Thank you," they have a word—*Gracias* or *Grazie*—that captures the essence of the important transaction under way. You have done something for me, and for that I am grateful. "Thank you" works, but it seems to pale in comparison, especially when you consider all we've learned in recent years about the force you wield when you acknowledge that someone else's actions have improved your life. Gratefulness is linked to almost every other element of The Difference: optimism, resilience, connectedness—the list goes on. And that makes this a very important chapter to absorb.

MEET CLAIRE

AGE: Fifty-two
FAMILY: Single, no children
ASSETS: $2 million
CLAIRE'S DIFFERENCES: Grateful, resilient, optimistic

Claire's career with the San Francisco mounted police unit ended early when she was thrown from her horse and broke her neck and back. She now lives on a small inheritance, investments, a pension, disability, and careful planning—over the years, she never took on debt and was careful to save as much as her salary allowed. Despite her fall and the pain she still experiences daily, she says she's lucky— lucky to be alive, lucky she had the foresight to save, and lucky to have had the experience as a police officer. The feistiness that allowed her to become a mounted policewoman serves her well now.

Q: *Where do you live?*
A: I'm a native of San Francisco. I grew up here. My parents deliberately moved us to this area to keep us away from Haight-Ashbury. I grew up in a conservative Catholic family, so that negated being too wild.

Q: Were your parents wealthy?

A: Moderately. They ended up well-off but I never knew about it because they were children of the Depression. My father was always looking for that nickel. There were very strict rules in my house about money. I was taught that if you can't afford to pay cash, you can't afford it—whatever it is, except for a house. So I've never bought anything on credit.

Q: How did you achieve financial independence?

A: I had a good career. I saved. And I worked overtime to pay off my house, which turned out to be good because I was injured on the job and am on total disability now. I was a cop, a sergeant in the mounted unit. In fact, I was the first female sergeant in the San Francisco police force on horse. But a pit bull attacked my horse, I was thrown, and I broke my neck and back. I landed on cement.

I am a very lucky person, very lucky.

Q: How is your health now?

A: I have chronic pain. I deal with that. I swim every day. I have degenerative arthritis in the back, among other things. But I count my blessings. A couple of years after my accident, Christopher Reeve passed away from his. So I know how fortunate I am, and I'm grateful for that. I'm also lucky because I was financially secure. So throughout the problems—I went two and a half years without pay while the city settled my disability—I was able to keep afloat because of the way I had saved. When I hit my twenties, my parents gifted us a little money. I have two older brothers. I don't know what they did with theirs, but I took every share of stock and did dividend reinvestment. That's turned into a gold mine.

Q: Did you know anything about stocks?

A: I was raised to read the stock pages before I was raised to read. I follow my father's way—hang on when low, buy more and hang on. It will always turn to profit. And don't panic. I never panic. I rarely look at my portfolio.

Q: Are you saying you didn't trust the city government to provide for you?

A: I didn't want to count on that. I wanted to change the world, and I was working for the love of it. I always figured my stocks and savings would fund my retirement. I didn't want a handout—I wanted to save society. Money was a by-product, until I bought a house and then it was important. I guess I was raised to depend on myself. That's probably why I'm single, because I'm very self-sufficient. Even with my back problems, I'm very independent.

Q: How did you end up in the mounted police?

A: I just thought it would be more challenging. Being a lieutenant was more administrative, and I'm not administrative. I never thought I'd end up hurt.

Q: You're pretty gutsy.

A: Not really. I just believe you can do whatever you want to do. If somebody told me I couldn't do it, I'd do it. I was a sheriff first, and I had to go to the certified academy—this was in the '70s—and they told me no woman had ever done a pull-up. So I worked on it, and I did five—that was the requirement. I was the first woman to do pull-ups. It wasn't important to me to be the first, but because they told me I couldn't do it. I was raised to think you can do anything you want to do.

Q: If your parents hadn't given you stock, would you have started investing on your own?

A: Absolutely. But it's fair to say my parents' gift gave me a sense of security, knowing that it would be there.

Q: Would you credit your investments for your financial comfort?

A: I credit more what I said before—don't buy what you can't pay cash for. That stopped me from buying so much stuff, and then I ended up being happy I didn't buy it. I'll give you a good example. When I first got to the academy, they sent out a credit union representative and offered me a free car loan. I thought, "Wow, I'd like a new car." I went to my parents and we got into a whole discussion about debt, and that was the last time I ever thought about doing something like that. At the time my car was four years old. It was fine.

Down the road, I ended up buying this little Honda—it was brand-new. I never bought used, but I always paid cash. When I went to get a new car twelve years later because the Honda was giving me trouble, I bought an Acura. It turned out to be so nice, I kept the Honda because I didn't want to mess up the Acura. It's still in my garage, still smells of new leather. It only has forty thousand miles on it.

Q: What do you spend money on?

A: I bought a $2,000 TV yesterday; that's a big splurge for me. The old TV was from 1996. I took a cruise to Hawaii. Last year, I put an addition on my house. I have a little dog, and sometimes I have trouble taking her for a walk, so I had a contractor knock out a wall in my bedroom to build a deck.

Q: Are you always so positive?

A: I'm never not grateful, but on a bad day, I'm not so friendly. I always say, "What are you going to do?" I have a friend whose husband died of cancer last year at forty-nine. A year and a half later, she's still crying. Life's a crapshoot. You're given lemons, you have to make lemonade.

When I went for the horses over the desk job, my friends and family thought I was nuts. But I'd do it again.

CHAPTER NINE

Grazie

What is gratitude? What does it mean to be grateful? It means, certainly, to feel thankful. But new research argues that it is more than that. Gratitude can be a habit you practice like yoga, it can be an attribute—a part of your personality—like optimism, it can even be a moral code you adhere to in the same way that some people follow the Ten Commandments. And this new research—much of which comes our way thanks to leading researchers Robert A. Emmons, a professor of psychology at the University of California at Davis, and Michael E. McCullough, a professor of psychology and religious studies at the University of Miami—shows us that gratitude, like so many of the facets of The Difference, can be learned.

But before we get to that, let's look at the role gratitude plays in The Difference. Interestingly, people self-identify as "grateful" across the wealth spectrum.

Does "grateful" describe you very well?

	Yes
Wealthy	60 percent
Financially comfortable	59 percent
Paycheck-to-paychecks	54 percent
Further-in-debtors	58 percent

That may be because unlike "optimistic," "competitive," or other characteristics where as many as thirty percentage points separated the wealthy from the further-in-debtors, it's hard to live in this country, where even those who have very little have so much, and admit to *not* being grateful. But we saw greater differences between the groups when we look at gratitude from an action-oriented perspective.

Does the statement "I give back to the community as much as I can" describe you very well?

	Yes
Wealthy	35 percent
Financially comfortable	25 percent
Paycheck-to-paychecks	21 percent
Further-in-debtors	21 percent

And gratitude was an important factor for our movers.

In addition to its effect on wealth, gratitude is tied to many other benefits—both physical and emotional. Grateful people are happier, more optimistic, and healthier. They sleep more and exercise more, which puts them in a better frame of mind. Grateful people are less likely to be felled by depression or stress-based ailments. And they are likely to feel good physically. One 2003 study that asked people to count their blessings on a weekly basis for ten weeks found that people who followed through reported feeling healthier.

Attribute	Describes Me	Percent More Likely to Move Forward Than Those Who Said the Word Didn't Describe Them At All
Grateful	Slightly	16 percent
	Well	27 percent
	Very well	35 percent
	Completely	24 percent

Grateful people are more likely to be connected—in the way you want to be connected. They are more trusting of people they don't know, often viewing strangers as having good or relatively good motives ("relatively" is important—again, everything in moderation), rather than being suspicious of them. In the last chapter, we talked about "giving a little to get a little." Grateful people have this down. They give a little every day. And because they get a little back, they don't feel empty—or like they need to fill a void with unnecessary belongings.

In fact, Emmons and McCullough consider gratitude the antidote to materialism. Think about it. If you "want what you've got," you appreciate the value in the things, people, and benefits you already have. You know where they came from and are grateful that someone else likely provided you with these things at a cost to themselves. Materialism is just the opposite. It's focusing on what you don't have. It's obsessing on what you desire. This doesn't mean that grateful people are not concerned with wealth, assets, or generating income—they can be. It's just that their sense of identity is not as linked to these materialistic outcomes.

If you are grateful for what you have—if you thank the Lord, the stars, your spouse, and your friends for the good things they bring to your life every day—there's less room to be envious of what the Joneses are bringing into their lives. Or, for that matter, what they're parking in their garage.

Four Ways to Increase Your Gratitude Quotient

LOOK AT LIFE THROUGH A DIFFERENT LENS. Grateful individuals tend to see things as better—rosier—than people who are not grateful. And that perspective is reflected in the language they use. They talk about abundance. About how fortunate or lucky they are. About the gifts they receive on a daily basis. And they tend to believe they have more than they deserve. The not-so-grateful use a language of scarcity rather than abundance.

It's a very different mind-set, Emmons explains, and because the science is new, the language seems clunky as well. "When we think of something as a gift, we make more of an effort to protect it and nurture it. Even if we're thinking of something that we view as mundane—like our job—when we think of it as a gift, we focus on how life might be if we didn't have that job. And that makes us appreciate it more." So listen to the words coming out of your mouth and the conversations running through your head to pinpoint which one you are. If you're among the not-so-grateful, try to move the needle a bit using at least one of the following words every day: gift, giver, lucky, fortunate, graced, thankful.

STOP COMPARING. Emmons's research has shown that one of the things that makes a person grateful is a childhood in which he or she was accepted, nurtured, and loved for who they are rather than held up for comparison to all the other children in the classroom, neighborhood, or family. Chances are, if you grew up in a home where comparison was the model, you're still torturing yourself with constant measuring up today. Stop. The next time you catch yourself uttering or thinking the words "But he/she has _____" or "I wish I had _____," replace them with the words, "I am thankful for my_____." Over time, you will start to feel more complete.

USE VISUAL CUES. I have a sign in my kitchen that says THE MOST IMPORTANT THINGS IN LIFE AREN'T THINGS. It is one of several in my house—another simply says BREATHE—I use to remind myself of what's important. Why is this necessary? Because there are days when the dog throws up, the garbage disposal goes on the fritz, the car won't start (because I left the overhead light on again, aargh!), and my hair looks like hell. And although none of those things really matter, every single one can throw you or me off-kilter and make you or me forget to hug the kids on the way out the door. You don't have to post signs, by the way. Perhaps there's a landmark on the way to work that could be your trigger, or a picture on your desk. So much of not feeling grateful is simply forgetting, experts say. We need to remind ourselves not to forget.

DO SOMETHING FOR SOMEONE ELSE. Some people operate on the theory that in this world, we get what we deserve. Grateful people don't. They operate on the theory that they get more than they deserve. As a result, they are constantly doing things for others—often with no payback in clear sight—that make good outcomes happen. Grateful people tend to not only be more optimistic but more energetic, and that gives them the get-up-and-go to bring about positive outcomes. The trick is to simply start the ball rolling. A friend is having a particularly bad day? Place a phone call. Stop by to say hi. Pause to smile. No one is saying you have to spend three hours making a gourmet meal (although if you had the time, that wouldn't necessarily be a bad idea). The little things work just as well. And eventually—in unexpected ways—you'll get your karma kickback.

Fake It Till You Make It, Part III

As I write this, mortgage rates have spiked half a point, gas prices are setting new records on a daily basis, my children are off at camp, and I am missing them. I woke up at 5 a.m., took a shower, got dressed, climbed into the car to drive to the *Today* show, sat down on the set across from Matt Lauer, and promptly got bumped because the previous segment ran long. So I got up out of my chair, put a smile on my face, and said, "Thanks anyway." Is that how I really felt? Not necessarily. But expressing gratefulness, even when you don't feel it, is part of the program. It gets easier as you go along. And as I walked out the door I was told that my segment was rescheduled for tomorrow morning at the same time. And for that, I really was grateful.

YOU MAY WANT TO GIVE FINANCIALLY, AS WELL

There is—by the way—another financial tie to gratitude. Grateful people give more. They give more of their money, more of their time, and no doubt even put more of their belongings into the sidewalk box for Goodwill or the Salvation Army.

The trick is giving smart—making the biggest difference not just for your own psyche, but for the organization you're looking to serve as well. If you're like most donors, you probably spread your charitable contributions among several groups that you know or that your friends ask you to support. But when the request for help goes beyond the routine $50 or $100 check, or if you decide on your own that you'd like to do something a little more significant, how do you know your money is going to the right cause?

LOOK AT THE PROGRAM RATIO—BUT NOT EXCLUSIVELY. If you're a savvy giver, you know to look up how much of a charity's income goes to programs, as opposed to overhead. You do this by consulting websites like CharityNavigator.org or by looking over the IRS form 990 that the charity files, which is available at guidestar.org or on the charity's site. Look for the line that says "program expenses." The higher the so-called program ratio, the better job a charity is supposedly doing allocating, managing, or utilizing your money. It's a good initial barometer. But simply looking at that ratio, according to Katherina Rosqueta, who heads the Center for High Impact Philanthropy at the University of Pennsylvania, is not enough.

Why not? It doesn't show how effective a program is. A food bank, for example, may shell out a lot on its program, but how many people is it feeding? Ask these questions as well.

COMPARE ORGANIZATIONS THAT HAVE SIMILAR MISSIONS. Mutual fund investors, particularly those schooled by Morningstar and its "style boxes," know that you don't compare apples and oranges. You compare funds that invest in growth stocks with other funds that do the same, or value with value and small cap with small cap. Do the same here. The worst food bank spends 90 cents of every dollar on its programs because, basically, there are no administrative costs. Yet it's rare to find a museum that spends more than 75 cents on the dollar because museums need guards, insurance, and big buildings. So look at how one food bank compares with another, not how a food bank compares with a museum. Finally, there's the issue of CEO pay. Charities have to disclose CEOs' compensation, as well as that of other highly paid employees. (It's on the 990.) Again, compare groups that have similar missions and staff sizes.

GIVE NEW ORGANIZATIONS A BREAK. Charities less than two or three years old shouldn't be evaluated on the basis of program ratios because their start-up costs are, by definition, overhead. Consider other data hiding in plain sight. One reason givers rely on the program ratio is that it's easily available. But there are other data points on the 990 that are just as important. Revenue growth combined with growth in spending on programs from year to year signals a financially healthy organization, for example.

GET PAST THE SALES PITCH. Fund-raisers will often tell you how important your donation is, and spend a fair amount of time buttering you up. Their job, after all, is to get you to open your wallet. Your job is to make sure that your dollars are doing the most good. You want answers to such questions as "What are this group's goals for the year?" "How will it reach them?" and "What's the measure of progress?" Well-run organizations welcome these questions. You're searching for anything that gets at cost effectiveness. If a program is aimed at reducing an area's high school dropout rate, has it worked? And how much did it cost to achieve that reduction?

Bottom line: The impulse to give comes from the heart. But the actual giving? As you would with any investment, use your head.

Exercise: Start a Gratitude Journal

Gratitude journals are not new, but we are starting to see more of their benefits with each passing year. According to Emmons's research, individuals who keep gratitude journals sleep a half hour more per night than those who don't, they exercise one-third more each week than those who don't, they're 25 percent happier than those who don't—and they tend to become people magnets. Although keeping a journal is a private exercise, the people who journal become more enthusiastic and pleasant to be around during the process. Their relationships are more rewarding, which leads to all kinds of success.

So what do you do? Grab a notebook or open a new file on your computer. Once a day for no more than five or ten minutes, systematically write about the things that you are grateful for. Explain why you're grateful in as much detail as possible.

In the beginning, you'll likely focus on concrete tangible things—your car, apartment, iPod. Eventually, you'll see a gradual shift toward more intangibles. You'll start to think about relationships that you value and ways others have done things that have been for your benefit. You may even find gratitude for life itself.

A Quick Guide to Chapter 10

Over the past few years, the country has been taken with the notion that working smart, or working ultraefficiently, is far better than working hard. In fact, most of us need to work both smart and hard to make The Difference. In this chapter, you'll learn about grit—and whether or not you have it. You'll see how your tendencies to put in the hours (or not) measure up to the population around you. You'll learn how to find the gumption to dig into a particular project even when you don't quite "feel it" in your soul, and why—at particular points in your life—this is a necessary skill to have. And you'll see why competitiveness (say it with me, "in moderation") is absolutely, positively a good thing.

MEET DON

AGE: Sixty
FAMILY: Married, two children
ASSETS: $1 million to $2.5 million
DON'S DIFFERENCES: Connected, hardworking, resilient

Some people look for shortcuts in life. As students, they want to leave class early, and to escape the office whenever possible as adults. Those thoughts didn't often cross Don's mind. He not only worked during work hours but also after work and on the weekends. And he tried to never—ever—use the word "no." It served him well.

Q: *Where did your money come from?*
A: Through investments, a 401(k), and work. We have a financial adviser who's been watching our dollars for a long time—thirty years, I betcha. When we were younger, we could aggressively invest. As we got older, we still do some aggressive investing, but also some not so aggressive.

Q: *How much input do you have?*
A: A lot. I told him my wife and I were poor when we were young,

and we do not want to be poor again. I guess that's why he watches our money so well—because I threatened him. [Laughs.] Whenever there's a bump in the market, I ask him, "Do we need to do anything?" He says we're fine. We lost about $5,000 last year, not much. But it wasn't our savings—it was money we'd earned off of our investments. It's a hit, but knowing that softens the blow somehow.

Q: Let's go back. Tell me how you got to where you are today.
A: My wife and I both worked for a telecommunications company. We both had 401(k)s, and we put a lot in to get that free matching money. We started contributing to them when we first became eligible. That was 1980-something. Before that, we were saving in credit unions or whatever.

Q: Did you go to college?
A: No, I took some classes but never got a degree.

Q: How old were you when you got married?
A: We got married in 1965—I was going to be eighteen, my wife was eighteen. We were high school sweethearts. We have two girls, the first within the year after we got married. We had the second one ten years later.

Q: I assume you struggled at the beginning?
A: Oh, yeah.

Q: Was there a turning point?
A: A turning point of saving money? We saved all our lives. My wife is good at cutting corners. But I suppose there was a turning point when we moved from Colorado to Arizona. When we moved, we didn't go anywhere, didn't know anyone, and didn't spend any money. We just concentrated on saving our dollars and buying a house. We moved here in 1969.

Q: You said you were poor. Was that a great motivator?

A: Sometimes we had no food. I was raised by my mother. She didn't have an education, and there were a lot of kids in my wife's family and in mine—eleven in each. There were seven boys and four girls in my family.

Q: Did you know you were poor?

A: I always knew, by watching some of my other siblings, that I wasn't going to be able to do some things. When I went to school, some of the kids were making plans to go to college, and I was making plans to finish high school.

My parents lived payday to payday, borrowing whenever they could. They lived beyond their means. I used to say, "I'm not going to struggle like that. If I can work hard, I know I can make money."

Q: Where did you get that idea? It doesn't sound like you had a role model.

A: I don't know. I didn't get it from my dad. But I spent time watching successful people. I come from a farming community. Friends would work hard and be rewarded for that work. They always had nice clothes and nice houses. I didn't come from a farm, but I thought if I can work hard, and put in as many hours as I can in a day, I can be successful.

Q: What was your idea of successful?

A: I used to tell my kids, whatever I have and I am, I worked hard for. Kids who go to college—get an education and a degree—go far. And they did. My daughter is very successful; well, both are. They have better-paying positions than I could ever get.

Q: How did you do in school?

A: So-so. School wasn't my favorite thing. When I was in junior high and high school, I always had a job that contributed to the family.

Q: Do you think moving away widened your vision?

A: Yes, definitely. I always used to say, "If only I could live in a big city." I figured there were more jobs and I could work three jobs if I wanted to. I used to work two. In my hometown, you were lucky to get one job. I'd go into homes and hang their window coverings—drapes, curtains, everything custom-made. I worked after work and on the weekends.

Q: Did you mind it?

A: No. I think once a week I went to a class—accounting class. I wanted to get some education. As I got older, I thought I could learn more.

Q: It sounds as if you were self-conscious about not having more education.

A: I know at some point I was self-conscious, I wished I had more education. I think my career would have gone faster. A few years before I retired, though, I was lead project manager at my company. At meetings, everyone would go around the room and introduce themselves and say I have a master's from here, I have a degree from there, et cetera. I would say I have some college classes. And I would think, "And they all report to me."

Q: How did that happen?

A: I networked well and aligned myself with people who could help me, and I belonged to a mentoring program through the company. I was mentored. That gave me perspective about how corporations work—how to interview, the pitfalls and successes.

I always tried to treat everybody the same, no matter what level they were at. That helped me out because that was how I wanted to be treated. No matter what level, with the everyday working people—because that's what I once was.

Q: Did you always know you'd climb the career ladder?

A: I always wanted to. I remember being asked what I wanted to do by one of the managers. And I said, "I want to do a good job so you'll get promoted and then I'll get your job." And I did get the job.

Q: Why did you keep getting promoted?

A: I did hard work, a thorough job, and very seldom said "no" to anybody. I always said something like, "That might be difficult, but let me look into it."

Q: So what do you do now?

A: Travel. We travel wherever we can. Back when we were raising the family, we seldom went anywhere. Now we have trust money set up, and we can go wherever we want and not have to worry.

CHAPTER TEN

Working Hard *and* Working Smart

Let's talk about what it means to work hard. Does it mean you put in the hours—more, say, than the guy or gal at the next desk? Does it mean working until the work is done? Or getting more done in the same amount of time? Yes. To all of the above. And it is necessary for success and necessary for wealth even more so in recent years when job security is limited. Our research bears that out.

Does the term "hardworking" describe you very well?

	Yes
Wealthy	72 percent
Financially comfortable	69 percent
Paycheck-to-paychecks	68 percent
Further-in-debtors	67 percent

These are notably slimmer differences than we saw for other measures like "optimism" and "resilience." But, notes Duke University finance scholar David Robinson, nobody wants to admit they're *not* hardworking, no matter what category they fall into. He's got a point. The percentages of people who say they identify "very well" with the word "hardworking" were higher than for any other personality trait. "Multitasker," which some see as a euphemism for "hardworking," was a close second. (More on that momentarily.)

And, of course, given our economic times, working hard (or at least being perceived as doing so) has a considerable upside. "In the U.S., where there is limited job security, the extra hours that you can put in really count for something," says Harvard University economics professor Richard Freeman. "What we've seen is over the last four or five years, with computers and then home computers, Internet connections, and cell phones that actually work, is that white-collar people who tend to be successful are working another eight hours that the government never counted. You work at home on the weekend. You work at night after you leave the office. I think if anything with the current economy, this is just going to continue, because no one wants to be the one who gets laid off."

It's not just white-collar workers, Freeman goes on to note. Self-employed people work longer hours, in part because they get to keep the rewards from their work. People who work from home put in longer hours, in part (I say from experience) because we don't want those still in the office to think we're slacking off. Even young workers, Freeman points out, know the drill. Say you're running an ice cream store, and you have kids working there. "If you're the manager, you know the really tough climb is Saturday night, when teens would rather be out with their friends. So the one who comes in on that Saturday and does the job and puts in extra time or stays an extra shift, that counts incredibly. It just looks good to be available."

And indeed, our research reflects that as well. David Robinson took a look at the data to isolate the additional hours worked by people who—no matter what category they fell into—said they identified with the label "hardworking." Individuals who said they were "slightly" hardworking put in an extra 1.4 hours a week more than people who didn't identify themselves as hardworking at all. Those who identified with the label "well" put in an extra 3.1 hours, "very well" an extra 4.9 hours, and "completely" an extra 7.4 hours.

Why is it, though, that some people work harder than others? Why is it that some teens are willing to scoop double chocolate chip on a Saturday night when others aren't, or that some executives put the kids to bed then put in a second shift at the computer, rather than let the company down? Where does that drive come from?

Conscientiousness and the Big Five

In the years after World War II, psychologists started to wonder if there was a way to organize the almost infinite number of ways that human beings differ from one another. It seemed to those working the puzzle—led by two independent research teams—that those multitudes of differences had certain links. For instance, a person who is sociable is also likely to be somewhat assertive, energetic, and positive. By the late '60s and early '70s, the researchers had determined that all personality traits, in fact, could be lumped together by their similarities into five larger personality buckets: extroversion, agreeableness, conscientiousness, emotional stability, and intellect. These buckets, or groups of traits, became known as the Big Five.

Working hard falls into the conscientiousness bucket. But before we discuss what it is and why it's so valuable, let's ask the pertinent question: Do you have it?

How Conscientious Are You?

Here are a number of characteristics that may or may not apply to you. Place the appropriate number, 1, 2, 3, 4, or 5, next to each statement listed below to indicate the extent to which you agree or disagree with the statement.

1 = Strongly disagree
2 = Disagree

3 = You are neutral about the statement

4 = Agree

5 = Strongly agree

1. Am always prepared.

2. Pay attention to details.

3. Make a mess of things.

4. Get chores done right away.

5. Leave my belongings around.

6. Often forget to put things back in their proper place.

7. Shirk my duties.

8. Follow a schedule.

9. Like order.

10. Neglect my duties.

11. Am exacting in my work.

12. Waste my time.

13. Do things according to a plan.

14. Continue until everything is perfect.

15. Make plans and stick to them.

16. Do things in a halfway manner.

17. Find it difficult to get down to work.

18. Leave a mess in my room.

19. Love order and regularity.

20. Like to tidy up.

To score: Score numbers 1, 2, 4, 8, 9, 11, 13, 14, 15, 19, and 20 according to the scale. Score numbers 3, 5, 6, 7, 10, 12, 16, 17, and 18 in reverse: 1 = 5; 2 = 4; 3 = 3; 4 = 2; and 5 = 1. Then add up the numbers.

Interpreting your score: Just like answering direct questions about whether you are hardworking brings out a bias in respondents (we don't like to acknowledge it if we are not working hard), many of these items do as well.

> *The highest possible score is 100.*
> *At 85 or above, you are very conscientious.*
> *At 70 to 85, you are about average.*
> *Below 70, there's ample room for improvement.*

It's Called Grit

So, what is it—exactly—that we're measuring? Conscientiousness encompasses traits including being punctual, ambitious, and orderly, as well as two factors that deserve elaboration: competitiveness and something that University of Pennsylvania psychologist Angela Duckworth calls "grit." When you have grit, you are a hard worker. You have stamina and are able to persevere to achieve your long-term goals. You are focused, dedicated, and disciplined. You finish what you start, even when you're down. You are Michael Jordan in Game Five of the 1997 NBA Finals, racked with a stomach virus, told by your trainers you're too sick to play. And yet, you not only do it anyway, you score thirty-eight points and win the game.

Grit is a desirable quality. Why? Because, as Duckworth explains, it's predictive of getting good grades, staying out of trouble with the law, living longer, and—to our point—succeeding on the job. Which, of course, leads to financial success.

Interestingly, Duckworth came to study grit because she—very much like me—wanted to know why some people, with talents being equal, became more successful than others. The work of Sir Francis

Galton, half cousin of Charles Darwin, pointed her in the right direction. Galton was knighted in 1909. He produced the first weather map and created the statistical concepts of correlation and regression to the mean, and was thought to have the highest estimated IQ ever. He observed that a trinity of traits distinguished extremely accomplished individuals. "The first was talent, the second hard work, and the third was zeal," Duckworth explained. "My interpretation was that those last two components enabled you to keep going despite all setbacks. That made sense to me."

I agree. Think about it this way: What do you get when you don't have grit, hard work, zeal? A person who skips around without finishing much of anything. A dilettante. Is that person a success? Not likely, because when you hop from one endeavor to another, it quickly becomes obvious that you'll never become a master of anything—or ever hope to rack up much of a balance in your 401(k). In her research, Duckworth asked a question similar to the one we asked in our survey about how grit dovetails with the number of career changes an individual has undergone. She found that the people with the most grit change careers less often, just as we found that people who change careers less often are more likely to embody The Difference and find their way to wealth.

Practice, Practice

If I were to rewrite the old Carnegie Hall quip (One man stops another on the streets of New York to ask directions. "How do you get to Carnegie Hall?" he asks. The other replies, "Practice, practice."), substituting "The Difference" for the prior destination, the answer might very well be the same. Yes, some people are born with more drive than others. Birth order itself even plays a role. If a firstborn child is highly driven, the sibling that follows is likely not to be. Why? Because he or she has to establish a different identity in order to thrive. You see the same sort of differentiation even in identical twins.

But working at grit, practicing it, is key. K. Anders Ericsson, a psychologist at Florida State University, is the world's leading expert in the study of experts. His body of work supports the notion that in order to become truly great at anything—a bona fide expert—you need to put in ten years of work. Ericsson believes that becoming great at something isn't necessarily something that you're born to do. "These people don't necessarily have an especially high IQ," he wrote. "[But] the one thing they always have is this incredible investment of effort."

Ericsson and his colleagues even broke down the numbers. They took a group of twenty-year-old violinists, asked conservatory teachers to judge their performances, then ranked them by the hours of "deliberate" practice they'd put in over their lives. The best averaged 10,000 hours; the second tier 7,500; the third tier, 5,000; and so on. What is deliberate practice? That during which you're focusing on your own weaknesses and asking for constant feedback to make yourself better.

Now, you may not want to be a concert violinist. You may not want to be Bobby Fischer, who put in a full nine years of deliberate chess practice before he became a chess grandmaster at the ripe old age of sixteen. But you want to be good enough at what you do to be amply rewarded for doing it. You want to have the fortitude to stick with something that—in the moment—is frustrating you to no end. How?

FIGURE OUT WHAT "IT" IS. Understand, just because you are motivated by something that doesn't motivate others—or which society has deemed an improper motivator—doesn't make you wrong. Money, for example. As we discussed in chapter 4, for some people money is the motivator that makes the difference. If that is what gets you up in the morning, so be it. But if solving the mysteries of autism lights your fire, or helping thirteen-year-old girls navigate the territory that comes with being a thirteen-year-old girl does it for you, that's fine, too. In essence, figure out what you want.

Steven Reiss, a professor of psychology and psychiatry at Ohio State University, has studied more than six thousand individuals. His work shows that there are sixteen basic motivators that influence all meaningful behavior. Some, such as honor and idealism, are tied to moral codes. Others, such as eating, exercise, social contact, and romance, are entwined with our more animalistic natures. Still others, such as power, independence, and saving, are—in a sense—euphemisms for money. None, he points out, are wrong.

WHICH LOCK WILL YOU OPEN? For some people, finding their motivator—or motivators—takes more time than it does for others. "Everyone is born as a key," explains Dean Keith Simonton, vice chair and professor of psychology at the University of California at Davis. "This key undergoes some modifications through life. The basic form of it is established at birth. In childhood certain parts are filed down, but sometime in late adolescence you start fooling around, trying to figure out which locks—and there are always more than one—you will unlock. Some of us are fortunate enough to find a lock early. Others embark on a search that leads to a few locks before they stumble on what's right. Still others might not find it until middle age, at which point they quit their job and do something different." That, in fact, may be the upside of a midlife crisis.

What if you desperately want a lock that your key won't open? It happens. The nice reality about ambitious goals is that people who choose to set them have a greater likelihood of actually reaching them. But sometimes we want things we may not be able to have. Relatively short aspiring NBA stars point time and time again to the example of Mugsy Bogues. He was five foot three—and phenomenal. But there was only one of him. Might you be the next? Sure. But you can also take heart in the fact that—eventually—another motivator will overtake you. Perhaps you'll discover that even more than playing, you love to coach.

PLAN A FUNDS PLAN B. There are two important lessons to take from this section. The first is that every person has a passion (or three) waiting to be unlocked. The second is that you simply can't afford to wait to start working—and working hard—until you find it. While you are test-driving various ideas and opportunities, you need to have some sort of career or profession or job with potential for growth where, even though you have certain reservations about it, you go ahead and do it. You pour yourself into it and you aim to succeed. You can't know what you'll unleash until you go for it wholeheartedly.

This entails organizing your life in terms of a Plan B that goes beyond this month, or even this year. It means recognizing that working in a job or succeeding in a career that you might not love provides you with stability, benefits, and—yes—money to support your family and your nonwork passions. It also gives you something more important: financing. If and when you find your true calling, you'll need resources to do it. That argument should be part of the motivating, internal conversation you have with yourself. "I'm going to use Plan A to fund Plan B, once I figure out exactly what Plan B is going to be."

TEST-DRIVE MOTIVATION AND PERSISTENCE. It is difficult for people who have never had the experience of working really hard toward a particular goal—or in pursuit of a particular career—to know when they're doing it, which is why work probably isn't the best place to look for the sensation the first time. Running a 10K, on the other hand, might be. People who set a sports-related goal push through obstacles, experience and recover from setbacks, and try to exceed their personal bests. If you're not an athlete, take up a musical instrument and challenge yourself to perform. Or learn a new art form with the intent of exhibiting your work at an upcoming show. Start with something small. Move on to something more ambitious. Then tackle something really substantial. "There are lots of things we can do where we know we really won't have a future," Simonton says. "But accomplishing them and overcoming any anxiety that comes along for the ride gives us a degree of motivation until we find that thing that we really do want to be our future."

EVENTUALLY, THE REAL WORK GETS EASIER. Once you have the hang of it, you apply the same sort of rigor that you'd put toward completing a triathlon or becoming a potter toward your work. You do it on a schedule. Every day. With focus. And with the understanding that it will—without a doubt—get easier. That's the way the brain works.

How? Let's go back to Bobby Fischer for a second. One of the things we know from studies of chess masters is that their brains eventually compress the moves of the game. Where you or I or other people who play amateur chess might see the next smart move, Bobby Fischer and other experts see a sequence of ten coming down the pike. It's a maturation of the brain called "myelination"—where new connections develop—and pruning—where those synapses that aren't needed are, essentially, deleted. These sorts of brain changes don't just happen in chess prodigies. They happen in accountants, lawyers, entrepreneurs, and anyone who takes the time and makes the effort to become truly proficient at something.

GO WITH THE FLOW. Some of us have been fortunate enough to feel "flow." That's the term Mihaly Csikszentmihalyi coined for the experience of getting so caught up in an activity that you lose track of time. You forget to eat or even to go to the bathroom. When you look up hours later to see that the entire day has "flown" by, it is both hard and easy to believe. You need a little taste of this in your work. Not every day, but certainly from time to time.

Competition Brings Out Our Best

There is a final factor that brings out our desire to work hard, which is without a doubt tied to both wealth and success: competitiveness. Studies have shown that most people perform better when they have something or someone to beat. You can see a huge discrepancy in this quality even between the financially comfortable individuals we surveyed and the wealthy ones. The wealthy readily admit their competitiveness.

Does the word "competitive" describe you very well?	
	Yes
Wealthy	57 percent
Financially comfortable	38 percent
Paycheck-to-paychecks	29 percent
Further-in-debtors	27 percent

Competition appears to have been something their parents priori-tized. Of the wealthy individuals we surveyed, 59 percent said they were raised competing in team sports, such as soccer or basketball—a significantly greater number than participated in individual sports, such as gymnastics or karate (42 percent), or even creative lessons such as art or music (44 percent).

Competitiveness is more acceptable and more apparent in men than in women—not just in our survey, but in many others that have come before. It may be the one factor that, more than others, keeps women from reaching their potential. It's not that women are not as competent. It's that when there is a choice between solving a problem in a competitive setting or a noncompetitive one, men are twice as likely as women to opt to compete.

Economics professors Muriel Niederle of Stanford University and Lise Vesterlund of the University of Pittsburgh studied forty men and forty women who had been previously shown—in a noncompetitive setting—to have the same ability to complete a fairly basic math task. The researchers then asked the subjects to complete the task again but this time to choose whether they'd like to compete. Seventy-three per-cent of the men opted to compete; only 35 percent of the women did. Why? Men are overconfident. They think they will win more than they actually do. But the fact that they enter the fray gives them a chance to win. The fact that women don't essentially disqualifies them from vic-tory. To win, you need to throw your hat in the ring—that's just as true when a promotion is on the line, as when the race is a one-hundred-yard dash.

So what can you do to compete in a way that will best serve your goals of wealth and success?

EYES ON THE PRIZE. Make sure that the goals you have are performance goals, not outcome goals. Think about a classic "keeping up with the Joneses" example: Your next-door neighbor plants a new Lexus in the driveway and you are overwhelmed with thoughts of how you want one, too. If you get too focused on that outcome, you'll lose sight of what you need to do—day to day—to reach that outcome. The everyday tasks—exceeding your sales quota to boost your take-home pay, spending less on things that mean less to you—are your performance goals, and they are the ones that matter.

COMPETE AGAINST YOURSELF FIRST. What is your personal best? Filling a room when you give a presentation? Writing a brochure that's so good the first time the editor doesn't feel the need to send it back for revisions? Think about doing the best you can—rather than gathering a bigger crowd than the next guy's or writing a brochure that sings like your more seasoned colleague's.

STEP BACK TO MOVE THE BALL FORWARD. If competing against yourself in your current arena doesn't do it for you, acknowledge that. Then ask yourself what you need to do to put yourself in the arena in which you want to compete. You've been an accountant, but you really want to be a nurse practitioner? That means going back to school, taking a financial hit, and figuring out how best to do it all simultaneously.

THINK ABOUT WHO YOU ARE. All too often, being in the thick of competition means we sacrifice who we are in order to get what we think we want. It is possible to work hard—and compete hard—while maintaining your character and integrity. It just means monitoring yourself and the compromises you are making (compromises are almost always necessary) to get what you want. Are you sacrificing too much of your family life? Your creativity? Perhaps it's time to take a step back.

MAKE FRIENDS WITH FAILURE. At times you will fail. Let that knowledge help guide you, rather than define you. Let it validate that you're a worthy competitor—and then ask those around you for feedback. What worked? What did not? This is a strategic way of using your failure to your advantage. You can then tweak your skills, your process, or whatever is necessary to move you closer to success the next time.

TOOT YOUR OWN HORN. Finally, there are times you engage in competition—often on the job—when those who have your paycheck and review in their hands might not realize it. That's when you need to toot your own horn. It's critical that you understand how your performance is being evaluated. You need to be able to explain your own output in the supervisor's language. That means tracking your own production, taking good notes on what you accomplish, and using those notes at your next performance review. You're not bragging. You're explaining the value you bring to the organization.

Working Smart: Time Is Money

Of course, there are limits. There is a point at which working hard—or harder—ceases to pay off. There is a point at which putting in the hours becomes little more than banging your head against the wall.

For most people, that barrier is fifty hours per week. Some people can sustain sixty, but for most, once you top a fifty-hour workweek, you begin to show signs of wear and tear. Your temper shortens. Your stress level rises. What do you do then?

Stop. Ask yourself: How am I really spending my time? What activities are consuming more of my life than I actually think they are? Am I spending hours and hours unconsciously doing things that are not worth my time?

A story: A much-too-large chunk of my early winter was wasted trying to buy a wide-screen TV. After finishing my basement with the explicit goal of turning an empty concrete space into a Wii-playing, movie-watching, comfy-couch-laden rec room, I knew that the TV had to be really big and really flat, with good but not top-of-the-line picture and features. Easy enough.

I started online at ConsumerReports.org and CNET.com, then read a dozen or so reviews from magazines and newspapers. Now, more confused than before, I went shopping: Costco, Best Buy, Sam's Club, and Costco again, where I discovered that none of these sets would come close to fitting in my car.

Back to the computer, where I decided to let PriceSCAN.com, with its star ratings from consumers and search engine for the best prices (including shipping), have the final word. I settled on a fifty-eight-inch Panasonic widely available as I write this (though I'm sure prices will have dropped by publication) for around $3,000. And then I couldn't pull the trigger, wondering if there wasn't a better deal to be had—if only I looked some more.

It began to dawn on me that I had spent the equivalent of a full workweek searching for a bargain that might save me a few hundred bucks. Crazy, no?

But I have plenty of company. My friend Paige, a management consultant, tells the tale of "visiting" the Honda CR-V she wanted so many times that the salesman didn't believe her the day she arrived to finally buy it. And in this era of high gas prices, how many times have you heard of drivers heading across town or a state line to save $5 on a fill-up? Do they stop to consider the value of their time (not to mention the extra gas they burn on their journeys)?

I was in clear need of some perspective. And if these stories resonate, you likely need it, too. How do you get it?

KNOW WHAT YOUR TIME IS WORTH. We have a "vague sense of 'time is money,' but it's not telling enough for most people," says Timothy Ferriss, author of the bestseller *The Four-Hour Workweek: Escape 9–5, Live Anywhere, and Join the New Rich,* which argues that more efficiency allows us to cut way back on time in the office. "Only what gets measured gets managed," he says. But how do you measure? How do you know what your time is worth? Here's a quick and dirty formula: Say you make $50,000 a year. Remove the last three zeros. Divide the remaining number ($50) in half and you get your approximate hourly rate, in this case $25. If you make $100,000 a year, do the same thing. Lop off the zeros ($100), divide in half, and you get $50. Unless you're making that much in savings by shopping for your TV or combing the Internet for coupons (or whatever your time-suck happens to be), you're losing money.

LOG YOUR PURSUITS. It took me a while to realize how overboard I'd gone on my TV quest. I would have done better if I'd kept a time log. This works like a spending tracker, with a twist. For a month, record the amount of time you spend shopping, what you were looking for, your estimate of the original price, and the price you actually paid. If you put in forty hours for a $200 savings, you need to ask yourself: Is my time worth more or less than $5 an hour?

IS THIS FUN OR DRUDGERY? Do you like the activity that's eating up your time—or do you hate it? Doing lawn work, for example, may not be worth the effort judged strictly by your hourly rate. But there's value in exercise, in time spent outdoors, and in reclaiming a patch of green. Many people find it relaxing and fun. Likewise with shopping: For some people it's like raking nails across a blackboard. For others, it's a day at a spa.

One final insight: A big reason we tend to spend enormous amounts of time on tasks that provide minor payoffs is that we have a dearth of other activities we find compelling. What happens when you wake up on a Saturday morning, the kids are off at soccer practice, and you don't have anything scheduled? You check your e-mail (at least that's what I do), get lost online, or maybe watch some dull fare on television. The monetary benefit is nil, and the nonmonetary one isn't much higher. If this sounds like your Saturday, it's time to do a better job of scheduling activities you really enjoy, from exercising to dining out to listening to music. Just as we're better off when we watch how we're spending our money, we're better off when we watch how we're spending our time. It's the best insurance we have that we won't someday wonder how either one slipped through our fingers.

Exercise: Work Harder—and Smarter

For three days, keep a log of how you spend your workday. Every hour, pause to write down what you were doing, breaking that hour into fifteen-minute increments. (If after trying this for a day, you can't remember what you were doing forty-five minutes earlier, do your writing every thirty minutes instead.)

At the end of the day, go back over your log and give each fifteen-minute increment three ratings on a scale of 1 (lowest) to 5 (highest): the first for the satisfaction you took from the time, the second for whether the activity was "productive," meaning it generated a reward for you or your company, the third for whether the activity challenged you. After three days, go back and run a quick calculation of what percentage of your days were (a) satisfying, (b) productive, and (c) challenging. How much of your days rated 4s and 5s? (We're aiming for 80 percent.)

Then, over the next week, try to schedule yourself so that more of your time is spent on those satisfying and challenging activities. Delegate the things you ranked a 1 or 2 to others, or, if you are unable to delegate, allot yourself one or two hours at the end of each day to get those activities done. Eventually, you'll find you're spending more of your time doing the things you find satisfying, productive, and challenging. The people you work for and with will notice the improvement as well.

A Quick Guide to Chapter 11

There are two habits you must master in order to make The Difference in your life. The first is saving—for emergencies (so that when the roof leaks or the transmission goes out you don't need to finance the fix on your credit card), and then for the future. The second is investing—putting the money you save to work for you so that it multiplies enough to fund your retirement and other needs. We'll cover investing in chapter 12. In this chapter, though, we'll focus on the lost art of saving money. How much do you need to save? Where do you put money once you've saved it? But we'll start with the question so many people are asking these days: Why can't I save any money?

MEET DANNY

AGE: Twenty-nine
FAMILY: Single
ASSETS: $500,000 to $749,999
DANNY'S DIFFERENCES: Able to read other people, resilient, confident, passionate about work, habitual saver

Ever met a person who seems to work harder at saving money than they do at investing it—or even earning it? They're a dying breed. But Danny is one of those people. At the ripe young age of twenty-nine, he spends a good deal of energy thinking about how to save a buck on things like food, entertainment, dates, and clothing. He estimates that he puts away about half his salary; in fact, after finishing grad school, he continued to live on a student's budget despite landing a good job as a professor at a top-tier university. His motivation seems to come from the thrill of finding a good deal, rather than watching his savings add up—he says he checks his investments only once every few months, if that. And yet, it's a strategy that has made him financially comfortable, bordering on downright rich.

Q: How did you build your wealth?

A: I am a saver. My whole family is full of savers. When I got out of grad school, I had a little money, and I decided to live within the same means I had when I was in grad school. Since I was used to living like that, it didn't feel like deprivation. Since then I've become used to it, even though I'm making lots more money. I don't spend it, I invest it. I also had a small inheritance and parents who helped me through college.

Q: Were your parents wealthy?

A: We never worried about money growing up. If there was anything I needed, my parents made sure I had it. If I wanted a video game system, that wasn't going to fly, but if I needed a new textbook, I got it.

My whole family is fairly frugal, and so I grew up learning this from them. I know lots of people who buy music, which I never understood because you can get it for free on the radio. Why buy a book when you can get it from the library?

Q: Do you do things like go out for dinner?

A: Yes, but I find it cheaper than cooking for myself. I could make ramen noodles for almost nothing, but if you're single everything is packaged for families. I buy a whole cantaloupe and end up throwing out half. Also, it turns out, given my salary and schedule, if I make $50 an hour and I'm cooking, it's cheaper to go out than spend my time cooking. I wouldn't spend $50 on a meal. You also have to look at opportunity costs—what my time is worth. If I spend an extra hour working, I make an extra $50. If I can get that service taken care of for less than $50, that's a profit for me.

Q: What do you spend money on that's not a necessity?

A: Traveling to see friends and family, mostly family. I spend more than I need to on rent, but I choose to live closer to work for a shorter commute. So I probably make more on the extra time from the commute than I could make if I had to travel farther.

Q: You think of everything as a cost-benefit analysis?

A: Yes. I haven't bought a house because I would have to spend time on the care and maintenance of the house. And I'm single. Some people say it's a better investment to buy, but I think of the money for a down payment and the maintenance and how much I could earn by investing it. Once you run the numbers, I'm not sure the dominant option is to own rather than rent.

The other big thing is job security: I'm a junior faculty member. I'm going for tenure in two more years. Just 20 percent of people get the job, 80 percent get fired. So I don't want to put my time and money into a house if I'm going get fired in a few years. I'd like to think I'm good enough to get tenure, but it's impossible to know these things.

Q: Any indulgences?

A: I like cookies. That's probably my biggest. If I buy one package a week—chocolate chip are my favorite, maybe Chips Ahoy—that's my indulgence. The other thing is to have friends who bake.

But really, I don't spend my money. My friends say: "Let's do something. You have money, why don't you spend it?" But I don't like to get ripped off.

I'm not averse to seeing a Broadway show, but it can range from $30 to $200, depending on the seats you want. Some shows are worth it, some not. To be honest, this is going to sound really cheap—I prefer student shows to Broadway shows, because they're more fun. Talking to you, though, I feel cheap. I'll just call it frugal.

Q: When was the last time you spent money when you didn't want to?

A: On my last vacation, I spent $90 on a tour. But it was a spectacular tour—eight-thousand-year-old cave paintings—and I didn't regret it at all. The trip in general was something I wouldn't have done a few years ago, even after grad school, when I was trying to build up a nest egg.

Q: You started putting money away while still in grad school?

A: I realized if I could gather $50,000 at age twenty and not touch it, by the time I was sixty-five I could retire. In grad school, my stipend was $18,000, and I put away $4,000. That seems trivial but during the dot-com boom, stocks were doing real well and grew very quickly. I graduated in 2004 and my salary tripled and I was still living the same way, and saving over $50,000.

Today, I'm saving less of my salary, but my investments are pulling in more.

Q: Do you make your own investment decisions?

A: Most of my money is in mutual funds. I went to a couple of banks and insurance companies and looked at a bunch of funds and past performances and looked at those that didn't have ridiculously high yields but consistently mid yields. Then I invested in a couple of different ones in case one went sour.

Q: How often do you look at your portfolio?

A: I try not to look too frequently, so I'm not tempted to pull out. I look every few months.

Q: You mentioned an inheritance?

A: My grandparents left me stocks, which I haven't touched. My grandfather was a stockbroker and I figure he knew what he was doing. My strategy is to invest broadly and not touch it when you think you should—when things are going badly—because that's the worst time.

Q: Were you always so smart?

A: [Laughs.] I got rejected from every grad school I applied to. Eventually I was put on a waiting list at one and got lucky and got in. I developed my undergrad career centered on grad school. My whole self-esteem centered on getting into grad school, so that was extremely hard.

Q: Do you think you changed because of the rejection?

A: I became a much harder worker. I was prone to slacking off, and then I realized I couldn't rest on my laurels. Most of high school and most of college, I didn't have to work very hard. I'm a smart guy. But I was at a new level of competitiveness and had to learn to work harder— better to learn that then, before it was too late.

Q: I'm curious. You're a young guy. You're single. Does being this frugal hurt when it comes to finding a long-term, serious relationship?

A: I was in one once and it did tax my budget. It does cost some money to be in a relationship, but I'm not very lucky about relationships. My current location doesn't lend itself to success in romantic endeavors. I'm not allowed to date students, and that's all there is in my town.

Q: But have you found not spending to be an issue?

A: No, not really. When I want to do something in the evening, I'm in a university town and there are drama clubs and interesting speakers and sporting events and cheap seats. You can go to the less popular ones like rugby for free, and usually they're more fun anyway. I guess people think I'm creative when it comes to planning my dates. There are so many things to do when it comes to dating—you don't have to go to dinner and a movie. You can go on hikes, or free outdoor concerts in the park and bring a picnic, and it's always almost free and romantic.

Q: Do you expect to have more money in the future?

A: Sure. With the continuation of what I'm doing and when I get tenure, there will be an increase in salary. I know I sound very driven by money, but I could be making a lot more. I'm doing what I'm doing because I love it. If I needed to, I could double my salary at any point. So making more money is always there if I need it. I live very frugally and enjoy it. I don't understand people who spend $200 on a pair of jeans. I'm happy with my imitation brand.

CHAPTER ELEVEN

The Healing Power of Saving

"But I can't save any money."

It's an excuse I hear all the time. Sometimes, it comes in the form of a whine. Other times it's more defiant. Over the past few years, though, it has become more and more frequent, as Americans have started spending more than we make, eating up the equity in our homes, and borrowing from our 401(k)s. The statistics are dismal by any standard. The national savings rate in the United States is a negative number. And with the economy on the rocks, the situation has gotten worse.

The question is, Why? Why don't Americans prioritize saving? We certainly know that saving money—like eating broccoli and strengthening our cores—is good for us. Yet saving for tomorrow is still an unappreciated skill.

Except among people who know The Difference. People who know The Difference are savers. And it has made them rich. We asked the question: "What has been most important in helping you reach your current financial status?" For the financially comfortable, saving not only topped the list, it trounced the list. For the wealthy, it was a close second to sound investing—and those two line items roared ahead of every other option. Take a look at the results:

What has been most important in helping you reach your current financial status?	Financially Comfortable	Wealthy
Habitual saving	54 percent	55 percent
Sound investing	34 percent	57 percent
A high paying job	30 percent	39 percent
An advanced degree	18 percent	15 percent
Buying my first home	18 percent	11 percent
Getting married	17 percent	12 percent
An inheritance	14 percent	15 percent
Starting a successful business	6 percent	13 percent
A substantial bonus	5 percent	6 percent
Getting divorced	5 percent	1 percent
A lucky break	4 percent	4 percent

What does it mean to save habitually? It means putting aside money month in, month out. Money gets pulled out of checking so that it cannot be spent and moved into a money market account where it can become the basis of an emergency cushion. Money gets pulled out of paychecks and plowed into retirement accounts such as 401(k)s, 403(b)s, SEPs, Keoghs, and the like. Money gets put away for tomorrow rather than spent today.

How much money? Well, 10 percent of the money you take in is a fine place to start, particularly if you're under forty. If you're over forty and haven't saved for your future just yet, you might want to aim for 15 percent. This does not have to be as difficult as it sounds—particularly if you still have an employer kicking matching dollars into your pool. They are counted in the total. But I am getting ahead of myself. If you haven't been a habitual saver to this point—or even if you've been one but haven't saved as much as you'd like—there are some things about the saving process you need to understand.

Saving Will Set You Free

Why is saving so important? Several reasons. First, without a basic savings account—an emergency cushion—you get stuck in a cycle of debt and more debt. Think about it this way: You are driving along the highway in your steady, dependable sedan, the one that you've counted on to get you to and from work for the past five years. All of a sudden you notice the brakes don't have the oomph that they used to. So you take it into the shop and, yes, you need new ones. Along with several other nonnegotiable repairs. Total: $1,200. If you have savings, you pull out your plastic knowing that when the bill arrives you'll pay it off immediately. But if you don't? You layer that charge atop all of those already on your credit card bill, and the cycle of revolving debt begins—making saving impossible.

Second, if you can't save, you can't invest. And investing—whether you do it in stocks or bonds, real estate or commodities, or preferably some combination of the above (again, more on this in the next chapter)—is the only way to ensure that the value of your hard-earned cash keeps pace with inflation and taxes.

Third, saving is synonymous with peace of mind. When you save money, you are taking care of yourself and everyone who depends on you. You are saying to all of those people: "You matter and so do I, and so I am going to put having money in the bank ahead of all of those 'things' that we think we want, but don't actually need." I know from the research conducted for my book on financial happiness that people who manage to put away at least 5 percent of their earnings every month feel significantly better than those who don't. (That amount may not ultimately be enough to fund your retirement, but it's a start, and once you start you will feel empowered to save more.) It is for all of these reasons that Wharton professor Robert J. Meyer described the act of saving money as "healing." I could not agree more.

And fourth and finally, saving is your only road to financial independence. If you have money saved, you have power—to walk out of a bad job, a bad relationship, a bad situation. You very likely have the confidence that comes with having saved that money, as well.

Americans Are Terrible Savers

We have become dismal savers in this country. It wasn't always that way. The generation that came through the Depression saved money consistently. The national savings rate spiked in the 1940s and tapered off in the 1950s and 1960s a bit, but by 1984, it was still 10.8 percent. By 2005, it had fallen to a negative .5 percent.

This happened for several reasons. Saving is harder for more people than it has ever been before. The average household income in this country has held steady in the low to mid-$40,000 range for a good half decade, while prices have continued to rise. If you're having to spend a disproportionate amount of your income on food and gas, it's hard to save.

Unfortunately, just as saving was becoming harder, spending—particularly spending money you didn't really have—became easier. Although the credit markets have significantly tightened up because of the mortgage crunch, for many years it was simply too easy to get your hands on money to spend. The prevailing logic was this: Why save when you could not only get that hot tub—you know, the one the neighbors just installed—but pay for it with a home equity loan that is both cheap and tax-deductible?

More Fun Than Pulling Teeth?

Most intriguing, saving is, was, and always will be no fun. "Saving money," explains Jason Zweig, author of *Your Money and Your Brain*, "doesn't feel good." Think about it this way: Choosing to save is almost always opting for delayed gratification instead of immediate gratification. You can buy a new suit today or have a nice retirement twenty years from now. You can go out to dinner now or put the money into an emergency fund in case the transmission goes out— someday. What are you going to do in those situations? You're going to buy the suit or head to the restaurant. The allure of getting something good today is much greater than the allure of getting something years in the future—even if the reward in the future is bigger.

That's an allure you not only feel (if it's not clothes that make you go mushy inside, it could be technology or rare books), it's an allure neuroeconomists (a relatively new breed of neuroscientists) can literally see. In recent years, they have started using MRIs to view the brain in the process of making money choices. What they have found is that when something we want to buy comes into view, the pleasure center in our brain fires up. And when we actually get that item, we get a feel-good dopamine rush. Delay the availability of the item even a day and you have to make the reward considerably bigger in order to arouse the same amount of interest from the brain. Things way off in the future— like retirement—don't jostle the pleasure centers much at all.

"Humans, like most animals, have a strong preference for immediate reward over delayed reward. If you offer me $10 today or $11 tomorrow, I'll probably say I'd rather have the $10 today," Zweig explained to me. Even bigger numbers don't seem to make the difference. Financial experts like me routinely use what-if scenarios to try to encourage people to save more and at a younger age—the sort that say if at age twenty, you put $100 a month into a tax-deferred account earning 8 percent, you'd have more than $527,454 at retirement. If you waited until you were thirty to begin, you'd have only $229,338. The difference in wealth is striking, sure, but by Zweig's logic, this method probably isn't very effective. "A reward you get in the distant future has no emotional kick to it, it's just an abstraction," he says. "Even if you tell people you'll have a million dollars thirty years from now, we may be able to understand it logically, but our brain just doesn't get it."

This, of course, is perfectly rational. If tomorrow's reward is based on promises, which retirement is, the people making the promises might be lying: They might not be around twenty years from now or your goals might change. Many things could happen. You didn't have to come through World War II or even 9/11 to understand this logic. Our brains have an automatic preference for an immediate reward. And that—along with risk taking—probably comes from our ancient hunter-gatherer ancestors. Back in those days, food was scarce. Given the choice of eating now or maybe eating more later, the cavefolk who chose the latter very likely starved to death.

Overruling Your Lizard Brain

The problem with ceding control to our lizard brains is that saving is absolutely necessary, even more now than in the days of our father's or grandfather's company pension. Not just because pensions have been overtaken by 401(k)s that we are responsible for funding ourselves (and we are not, by the way, funding them particularly well—the average balance is less than $30,000), but also because our longer life spans require the money to carry us for more years. Then there is the danger that Social Security and Medicare are at risk. "One of the things that publicly we're trying to do is get people to think more about their retirement, and realize that some of the benefits currently going to the retired, like Social Security and Medicare, cannot be sustained," says Brookings Institution economist Barry Bosworth. "They better start saving to take care of some of those needs themselves."

So the question becomes this: Knowing what we know about our money and our brains, what mind games can you play to psyche yourself into saving more money?

VISUALIZE YOUR GOALS. Let's say you're thirty-one and you want to retire in twenty-five years. The key is to make the goal as concrete as you can. Pick your birthday circa 2033 as the date for your retirement goal. Then you ask yourself this: What do I want to do when I retire? Do I want a villa in Tuscany, a boat slip in Fort Myers, a condo in Waikiki, or a paid-off mortgage where I am right now? Of course, it's different for everyone. But you've made retirement tangible: You have the date. You have the goal. Then you give it a name. It becomes "The Villa in Italy Fund," for example. Put a little Frank Sinatra on your iPod or pictures of Tuscany or Umbria on your fridge—whatever reminds you of your goal. Take a manila folder and put all your account statements in that folder, and decorate it with postcards from your last trip to the Amalfi coast. Sounds corny? Sure, but what you're doing is building an emotional environment within which you can save. All of these things work together in harmony to help motivate you, and then when you see the pair of shoes, it will be easier for you to say to yourself, "This is a choice between the shoes and Italy." All of a sudden, you can leave the shoes in the store.

RALLY YOUR TEAM. Use your friends and family as a way to discipline yourself. Tell them what your goal is and then ask them to remind you if they catch you about to spend money on something you won't need. (Tell them you won't get cranky. This is a goal for you, and you'll appreciate the help.) You can even do this now on the Internet. Yale professors Dean Karlan and Ian Ayres launched a website called StickK.com that allows you to post your goal, notify your friends, and then set up a series of penalties if you fail to come through. It worked for both founders, who lost a significant amount of weight by pledging a significant amount of money if they didn't drop pounds. But you could use it to help you build an emergency stash, increase your contribution to your 401(k), or amass college savings for your kids.

CHUNK IT DOWN. One reason many middle-income families don't save is that they don't believe they can come up with big enough sums of money to do it effectively. The fact is small amounts can be quite effective. Start with a few dollars a day. If you can't do that, start with your change. It sounds trivial, but I've heard story after story of people who accumulated hundreds of dollars that way, realized they could do it, and worked harder to save even more. Then add an automatic transfer from checking to savings every month. Some banks are even willing to transfer money weekly if moving smaller amounts more frequently feels easier on your wallet.

Finally, recognize that the saving process heals. It makes you feel better—a better person, a better spouse, a better parent—to know that you have something put away for your future. Even putting away small amounts of money can have a calming effect on your financial soul.

The One Best Way to Save Money: Stop Spending It

So, beyond the psychology, how do you save the most money? By not spending it.

I am not being flip or sarcastic. I am totally serious. Saving money means making a conscious choice to not buy something and instead leave the money in your bank account—or your wallet—where it can grow into a little slush fund that will eventually become a bigger slush fund that you can eventually invest to fund your life's dreams and goals.

The only way to get there is to start tracking where your money is going today. This is a tedious exercise—I want to acknowledge that right off the bat. But you do not have to do it forever. Instead, for the next month, make a commitment to write down every dollar—every dime—that you spend and where it goes. You can do this by tucking a notebook into your bag or back pocket and being diligent about taking notes, or you can (as I do) get a receipt every single time you make a purchase, shove those receipts into your wallet, and load them into a log (pencil and paper or computer) every few days.

Either way, what you will have when you are through is a road map that shows you where all of your money has gone. I guarantee if you have never done this, you will be surprised. You may see that more of your money is going to pet supplies or random trips to the grocery store or other nonessentials than you ever thought.

Once you have this information, you have choices. You can decide that you are going to spend less on certain items. You can decide that you are going to save the money that you do not spend. And you can put it away—in a money market account earning a decent rate of interest (these change constantly, but you can get a list at Bankrate.com)—until you decide where to invest it for the future. More on that in the next chapter.

How Much Do You Need to Save?

Here's one problem that keeps people from saving. Figuring out how much you need—particularly for retirement—seems so complicated that many people don't bother to go through the steps to figure out what their number actually is. That's unfortunate, because if you don't figure out how much you're likely to need, chances are you're not going to save nearly enough. A new study from Hewitt Associates took a look at the projected retirement levels of nearly two million employees at seventy-two large U.S. companies. It concluded that fewer than one in five workers will be able to meet 100 percent of their retirement needs. Yikes.

The fact that we're living longer—and living healthier—isn't helping matters any. Financial advisers used to tell people that if you could save and invest enough to replace 75 to 80 percent of your final income, you'd have a comfortable retirement. According to the Hewitt study, that's nowhere near enough. They suggest men need to replace 123 percent of their final salaries per year and women need to replace 130 percent. Those are numbers that may be well out of many people's reach—but shooting for at least 100 percent is smart.

Why do you need so much to retire? Because that money has to last a great many years. Some 19 percent of men and 33 percent of women who live to age sixty-five will live to be ninety or older. That means they'll have to support themselves for another thirty or more years. We want to travel in retirement, to start new businesses, to take up new hobbies, and to do all of these things from the comfort of our own homes. We tend to forget that living at home means maintaining it. When the washer or dryer goes at age eighty-five, we need to buy a new one. And then there's health care. As for the premium for being a woman: Women live an average of seven years longer than men, the average woman still earns 81 cents for every dollar a man earns, and women tend not to invest as aggressively as men. Throw all of those numbers into the soup and women need to save even more.

The problem is, most people aren't saving enough to even get close to what we might need. According to the Federal Reserve, the average 401(k) plan balance owned by people age fifty-five to sixty-four is just $60,000. Yikes! So how do we figure out how much we need?

First, figure out how much you'll get from Social Security by running the Social Security Quick Calculator (http://ssa.gov/OACT/quickcalc). Once you're there, select the inflated (future) dollars benefits estimate, not the one that provides benefits estimate in today's dollars. What you'll see is that delaying Social Security from sixty-two to age sixty-six or sixty-seven can increase your monthly take by a good third. It's a strategy worth considering if you're behind.

Next, use one or more of the many retirement calculators on the Web. Pretty much every financial services firm has one. So does every financial magazine. I'd start with the Ballpark E$timate* put together by the not-for-profit American Savings Education Council (http://www.choosetosave.org/ballpark/).

If you're not online, you can use this fill-in-the-blank version of the Ballpark E$timate. The worksheet assumes you'll realize a constant real rate of return of 3 percent and that wages will grow at the same rate as inflation; however, it does provide the user an opportunity to take into account longevity risk—the amount living longer could potentially cost. If you're married, you and your spouse should each fill out your own worksheet.

1. HOW MUCH ANNUAL INCOME WILL YOU WANT IN RETIREMENT?
Figure at least 70 percent of your current annual gross income just to maintain your current standard of living; however, you may want to enter a larger number. See the tips below.)
$_____

---

* The Ballpark E$timate® worksheet was developed by the American Savings Education Council® and the Employee Benefit Research Institute®, and is a registered trademark of EBRI. Further details can be found at www.choosetosave.org. Used with permission.

TIPS TO HELP YOU SELECT A GOAL

70 percent to 80 percent: You will need to pay for the basics in retirement, but you won't have to pay many medical expenses, as your employer will pay the Medicare premium and provides employer-paid retiree health insurance. You're planning for a comfortable retirement without much travel. You are older and/or in your prime earning years.

80 percent to 90 percent: You will need to pay your Medicare premiums and pay for insurance to cover medical costs above Medicare, which on average covers about 55 percent of medical expenses. You plan to take some small trips, and you know that you will need to continue saving some money.

100 percent to 130 percent: You will need to cover all Medicare premiums and other health-care costs. You are very young and/or your prime earning years are ahead of you. You would like a retirement lifestyle that is more than comfortable. You need to save for the possibility of long-term care.

2. SUBTRACT THE INCOME YOU EXPECT TO RECEIVE ANNUALLY FROM:

Social Security: If you make less than $25,000, enter $8,000; between $25,000 and $40,000, enter $12,000; over $40,000, enter $14,500 (For married couples, the lower earning spouse should enter either his or her own benefit based on income or 50 percent of the higher earning spouse's benefit, whichever is higher.) −$_____

Traditional employer pension: A plan that pays a set dollar amount for life, where the dollar amount depends on salary and years of service (in today's dollars) −$_____

Part-time income: −$_____

Other (reverse annuity mortgage payments, earnings on assets, etc.) − $_____

Total: This is how much you need to make up for each retirement year: = $_____

Now you want to estimate how much money you'll need in the bank the day you retire. The worksheet assumes you'll begin to receive income from Social Security at age sixty-five.

3. TO DETERMINE THE AMOUNT YOU'LL NEED TO SAVE, MULTIPLY THE AMOUNT YOU NEED TO MAKE UP BY THE FACTOR BELOW.

Choose your factor based on life expectancy:

Age you expect to retire	Male, 50th percentile (age 82)	Female, 50th percentile (age 86)	Male, 75th percentile (age 89)	Female, 75th percentile (age 92)	Male, 90th percentile (age 94)	Female, 90th percentile (age 97)
55	18.79	20.53	21.71	22.79	23.46	24.40
60	16.31	18.32	19.68	20.93	21.71	22.79
65	13.45	15.77	17.35	18.79	19.68	20.93
70	10.15	12.83	14.65	16.31	17.35	18.79

$_____

4. IF YOU EXPECT TO RETIRE BEFORE AGE 65, MULTIPLY YOUR SOCIAL SECURITY BENEFIT FROM LINE 2 BY THE FACTOR BELOW.

Age you expect to retire:
At 55 your factor is 8.8
At 60 your factor is 4.7

+ $_____

5. MULTIPLY YOUR SAVINGS TO DATE BY THE FACTOR
BELOW. INCLUDE MONEY ACCUMULATED IN A 401(K), IRA,
OR SIMILAR RETIREMENT PLAN. IF YOU PLAN TO RETIRE IN 10
YEARS, YOUR FACTOR IS 1.3.

15 years your factor is 1.6
20 years your factor is 1.8
25 years your factor is 2.1
30 years your factor is 2.4
35 years your factor is 2.8
40 years your factor is 3.3

– $_____

Total additional savings needed at retirement: = $_____

Don't panic. We devised another formula to show you how much to
save each year in order to reach your goal amount, and this factors in
compound interest. That's where your money not only makes interest,
your interest starts making interest as well, creating a snowball effect.

6. TO DETERMINE THE *ANNUAL* AMOUNT YOU'LL NEED TO
SAVE, MULTIPLY THE *TOTAL* AMOUNT IN LINES BY THE
FACTOR BELOW.

If you want to retire in:
10 years your factor is .085
15 years your factor is .052
20 years your factor is .036
25 years your factor is .027
30 years your factor is .020
35 years your factor is .016
40 years your factor is .013

= $_____

It's important to understand that using Ballpark or any calculator or worksheet is not an exact science. What you're really doing is running scenarios. You can see what happens if you run the numbers working a little longer—or growing your money at a faster rate. Or if you decide—since your mortgage will be paid off and you don't like to travel anyway—you don't need (or will never get to) the 123 to 130 percent Hewitt recommends.

What If It's Not Enough?

So many people are behind when it comes to saving for retirement and other big goals that I would not be surprised if you go through this exercise and are blown away. Part of resolving that problem is a matter of saving more. The other part is making some other financial choices.

POSTPONE RETIREMENT UNTIL SIXTY-SEVEN. And don't take Social Security until that time. Putting off your payments significantly increases your monthly take-home by as much as one-third to one-half. (Note: If you did take it and are sorry, you can pay the system back and start over at a later date with larger payouts. This can be a very smart move if you can come up with the cash for repayment. Call the Social Security administration or go to SSA.gov for more information.)

MAXIMIZE RETIREMENT ACCOUNT CONTRIBUTIONS. Nearly one-third of people didn't contribute to their 401(k) plans in 2007. Of those who did contribute, nearly one-quarter didn't contribute enough to get the employer match. That's leaving free money on the table. Other mistakes? Waiting to join the retirement plan until after you've been at the company for a year or two. And . . .

DON'T WITHDRAW WHEN CHANGING JOBS. Nearly 45 percent of people withdraw money from 401(k)s when they change jobs. This is a savings killer and a *huge* mistake. It can cost you 20 percent of the balance in federal taxes and 10 percent in early withdrawal penalties. Ouch.

HABITS THAT HURT: SMOKING

By this point, if you don't know that smoking is hazardous to your health—well, there's nothing I can say to hammer the message home. Thanks to the DARE curriculum sweeping the country, my teens now think it's an evil along the lines of crack cocaine and far worse than cheating on your taxes. Research shows it's just as bad for your wealth as for your health.

Jay Zagorsky of the Center for Human Resource Research compared the wealth of people who smoke a lot to those who smoke a little and those who don't smoke at all. The findings were pretty stunning. A nonsmoker's average net worth is roughly 50 percent higher than that of a light smoker (less than a pack a day) and 100 percent higher than a heavy smoker's (more than a pack a day). That wealth gap goes up more than $400 each year that the smoker continues puffing.

It's not just the cost of cigarettes—although quitting gives you an instant opportunity to pour each $4 to $7 you would spend per pack immediately into savings. Just as being overweight ends up costing you more in life insurance, health care, and so on, so does being a smoker. Quit and you can eventually get a break on your rates.

How much could you save by not smoking?

Seven dollars a day = $213 a month = $2,555 a year.

Invest that amount every year in a tax-deferred account where it could earn an average 8 percent a year.

In ten years, you'd have $43,216.
In twenty years, $133,468.
In thirty years, $333,795.
In forty years, $778,450.

Know When to Hold 'Em

My work involves speaking to large groups of people about their personal finances. Over the years, I've been in front of hundreds of groups comprising hundreds of thousands of people in total—and I can tell you that nothing grabs their attention like talking about how we occasionally overshop. I can and often do ask a simple question about whether you have ever bought something not because you needed it, or even really, really wanted it but because you were tired or had a bad day or had an impulse or had a glass of wine and your defenses were down. The room, inevitably, erupts in nervous laughter as every single hand shoots up in the air.

Why? Because we have all been there and done that.

The key is being able to recognize when it is okay to buy something—and I am all for treating yourself to things you want, as long as the saving is taken care of and as long as you can afford it—and when it is not. And to do that you need to learn to ask yourself the following questions at each and every point of purchase.

> *Do I need this?*
> *What happens to me (and my money) if I do buy this?*
> *What happens to me (and my money) if I don't?*

Exercise: Putting It in Perspective

Just as you have learned to journal about gratitude and optimism, it is helpful to write down your expenditures. This is an extension of tracking your spending. For a month, as you write down every purchase, make a note of how that purchase makes you feel. Then go back a day or two later and log how long that feeling lasted. Finally, answer these questions: Worth it? Or not?

Soon it will be easier for you to decide where you need to and really want to spend your money—and where you need to save it.

A Quick Guide to Chapter 12

It's not enough to earn a decent living—or even a living that is beyond decent. The wealthy take those earnings and put them to work. Very specifically. In stocks. And if you want to get there, you need to do the same, while avoiding some of the classic mistakes stock investors tend to make. In this chapter, you'll learn how the wealthy work the markets to their advantage. (It's not as complicated as it seems.) You'll learn how to automate your investments to your advantage. Plus, I've provided an exercise you can practice to quiet your nerves if the market is on a roller coaster.

MEET JIM

AGE: Sixty-three
FAMILY: Married, no kids
ASSETS: $2 million
JIM'S DIFFERENCES: Resilient, hardworking, sets goals, optimistic

There are some people who leap in, headfirst, and hope all goes well. Others like to put everything in writing and follow specific steps to achieve their goals. Jim falls into the latter camp. He says he has a business plan for everything, from building his retirement home (with all cash!), to setting up his investments, to working in his retirement years. Throughout his life, he's set specific savings goals, never allowing himself to fall back on credit. Because of a lifetime of careful saving and investing, he was able to retire with a net worth of $2 million.

Q: *How did you gain financial comfort?*
A: Simple. My dad brought me up to always save and never buy anything without really thinking about it first to make sure it was necessary. All of my life I have always put saving ahead of spending. When I

retired at sixty, my wife and I had paid off both homes and had a net worth of around $2 million with zero debt.

You have to have a financial savings plan and stick to it. Many people fail to save only because they never set up a dedicated savings plan. I tell anyone who wants to save that the first thing you have to do is start, and like anything else, stick to it.

Q: What kind of work did you do that allowed you to save?

A: I held numerous jobs. When I was going to college, I worked in a factory during the day and went to school full-time at night. I started buying "E" bonds at work. In those days I made $3.65 an hour and bought a $25 bond every week. I had to go into the army when I graduated college, because they still had a draft back then. After, I went to work for L'eggs Products. I stopped buying bonds and started buying stock because, back then, Consumers Energy was paying a 20 percent dividend and I always reinvested my dividends.

Then I started a security alarm company. We sold, installed, monitored, and maintained all types of closed circuit television, burglar alarms, and fire alarm systems. When I started my business I had a little over $70,000 in cash.

Q: What percentage of your income did you put aside?

A: I always put at least 30 percent of my net [take-home] pay into savings or investments. Usually this amounted to a steady investment of at least $1,000 a month. My rule was that we would invest first. We bought our first home in 1976 with 5 percent down and three years later bought our summer cottage by cashing in our bonds for the down payment.

Q: What did you invest in?

A: I have always invested more in stocks than anything else. In recent years, we've adjusted this mix with the purchase of mutual funds. However, whenever I've sold any stock it was to reinvest in something else. For example, in 1996 we tore down our summer cottage and built our retirement home. I sold $25,000 in stocks to start the construction and then for three years we worked on the home only when we had cash available. We used my wife's pay to buy all materials and labor. After just three years we had invested $160,000 cash and had our lake retirement home paid in full.

Q: Any important financial lessons you've learned over the years?

A: People need to think long term when it comes to saving money. The real secret to accumulating wealth is to let your money become your employee and work for you. In other words, take advantage of compounding interest and tax-sheltered investments to grow your investments. Also, keep saving something—even in the worst of times. When I was in the army, they called this living at one rank below your current grade.

Q: How did you become successful?

A: I got a good education. Although I was told in junior high school that I would be lucky to even finish high school, I went on to get both a bachelor's degree and then a master's degree in business. I always gave 150 percent effort to any job. I didn't let the chance of failure hold me back from doing something new. And I always did my homework before jumping into a new venture.

One reason 80 percent of new businesses fail in the first five years is because of a poor business plan. When I went into business on my own, I had a detailed five-year plan that took everything possible into consideration for growing my business and getting the necessary resources to succeed. I also had the necessary skills (both in sales and management) to ensure success. If I didn't have the necessary skills, I would have either gotten them first or hired someone who did.

Q: What did you do with your business when you retired?

A: One of my initial considerations I had when I created my business plan was to also make an exit plan for when I was ready to retire. I made a right-of-first-refusal agreement with the firm I worked for prior to starting my business. They were in the same industry. When I was ready to retire, they would have the first option to purchase my business at a set price based on the monthly revenues at time of sale. And they did.

Q: Are you retired now?

A: Yes and no. I love being in sales, so in 2006 I became licensed to sell real estate. My business plan—I always have a business plan—was that I would give it one year and if at that time I wasn't generating sufficient income to offset expenses, I would go back into retirement.

Going into real estate sales turned out to be a bad move and after one year, I exited. Four months later I decided to try my luck as a financial representative for Michigan schoolteachers. I took the necessary courses to become licensed to sell annuities and mutual funds and am currently learning this business. My business plan for this is slightly different—as long as I enjoy working with people I will stay in this business. If that changes, I'll probably try something else.

CHAPTER TWELVE

Make Your Money Work for You

As this book was being put to bed, the stock market was at its most volatile point in decades. Stocks were down hundreds (if not thousands) of points one week and up hundreds (we were hoping for thousands) the next. That was when Warren Buffett, the chief executive of Berkshire Hathaway Corporation, penned an op-ed piece for the *New York Times*.

A simple rule dictates my buying: Be fearful when others are greedy, and be greedy when others are fearful. I can't predict the short-term movements of the stock market. I haven't the faintest idea as to whether stocks will be higher or lower a month—or a year—from now. What is likely, however, is that the market will move higher, perhaps substantially so, well before either senti-ment or the economy turns up. So if you wait for the robins, spring will be over.

I include his words here because it echoes a very important finding from the survey conducted for The Difference: The wealthy buy stocks.

To some extent, this entire chapter can be summed up in those four simple words. The wealthy buy stocks. As we come to the end of our survey, we asked one question in quite a few different ways. But each time the answer was the same: The wealthy buy stocks.

Which describes the way you view the stock market?

	Too risky for a large portion of my wealth	Worth the risk of a portion of my wealth because of the returns it can generate
Wealthy	34 percent	66 percent
Financially comfortable	55 percent	45 percent
Paycheck-to-paychecks	77 percent	23 percent
Further-in-debtors	83 percent	17 percent

Have you invested in stocks and/or bonds for retirement?

	Yes
Wealthy	61 percent
Financially comfortable	45 percent
Paycheck-to-paychecks	33 percent
Further-in-debtors	22 percent

As we saw in the last chapter, for the wealthy, sound investing was the number one factor in helping them reach their financial status. Habitual saving was number two.

In the end, to get wealthy you must do both. Saving, in and of itself, isn't enough. That's because saving implies keeping your money safe—in a savings account, a money market account, a certificate of deposit, or some other financial holding pen where it is guaranteed to be there when you come back for it, but where the slim returns you're able to generate likely won't be enough to keep pace with taxes and inflation, much less exceed them.

Far too many people stop at saving. Others try to dip a toe in the investing waters but make mistakes along the way. Why? The reasons are many, but they tend to revolve around the same thing: risk. Because we are fearful, we don't take the appropriate risks at the appropriate times. Because we are uneducated, we don't understand that there are sometimes just as many dangers lurking in our inaction as in our action. So, before I lay out my straightforward and—I believe—relatively simple approach to investing for your future, let's look at the hurdles that may prevent you from implementing this approach effectively.

Dealing with the Unknown

The world of money is divided into two distinct hemispheres. There's the black-and-white hemisphere, in which any question you ask has one right answer. *Which no-annual-fee credit card sports the lowest interest rate? Which insurer has the cheapest term life for a thirty-five-year-old nonsmoking male?* Then there's the other hemisphere, gray and indefinite, where questions have many different answers. *Should I buy the stock I heard about on TV? Why sell that mutual fund now? Is an annuity for me?*

It's in this half of the world that your investments live. That can be a problem. Life trains your brain to make decisions based on what academicians call "representative heuristics" and what the rest of us call "rules of thumb." This works just fine in much of life. Think of the weather. If the sky is darkening, you bring an umbrella. If it rains, you're covered. If it doesn't, no big deal.

But where investing is concerned, these rules often fail us. We see stocks with the price trajectories of a young Google, or yearling mutual funds on a personal finance magazine's "hot list," and we pounce. We forget that there's been only one Google—and that the year after many of those funds are burning hot they tend to cool off quite dramatically. We fail to remember that in the history of the market, one year, three years—even five years—is too short a period of time to be a reliable indicator. And even our smartest money minds are guilty of it. When Alan Greenspan talked of a new economy after three short years of data on Internet productivity, he did precisely the same thing.

And even when our rational selves do remember that, for example, Google was an anomaly, our human nature (those lizard brains again) drags us back into the fray. It's like dieting. We know perfectly well we shouldn't order dessert when we're trying to lose a few pounds—or even allow the bread basket to be put on a restaurant table—and yet we do it anyway.

If you can understand the very traps you are likely to fall into—the specific mistakes that you are likely to make—you have a much better shot at becoming a successful long-term investor. This involves taking a look at your own tendencies as well as at society's as a whole. It's not necessarily a comfortable mirror, but if it saves you—or your retirement—it will have been worth it.

THE MISTAKES WE MAKE

WAITING TO BEGIN. There is, was, and always will be another—more pressing—use for your money than putting it away to grow for the future. There will be the car you want to buy, the house you want to paint, the vacation you want to take. And because they will all be here much sooner than, say, retirement, they will look much more enticing than a deposit into your 401(k) or IRA. But following your impulses on any of these other expenditures robs you of the most valuable commodity you have—time.

Witness: Invest the same sum of money, let's say $200, month in and month out until you retire at age sixty-five, in a tax-deferred portfolio earning 8 percent.

If you begin at age twenty-two, at sixty-five you will have $901,155.

If you begin at thirty-two, at sixty-five you will have $389,507.

If you begin at forty-two, at sixty-five you will have $258,998.

You may be inclined to argue, "What if I wait until age thirty-two to begin, but invest more money? Say, $300 a month instead of

"$200?" You'll have $584,261. Or $400? You'll have $779,015. In other words, you could invest double the money for the rest of your working life and still not catch up.

(You may also be inclined to point out that this is precisely the same sort of example Jason Zweig said human brains don't take as seriously as they should. For the record, I think Zweig is probably right on this—he is right on most things. But you can't blame me for trying. So defer a little gratification. And get going.)

NOT DIVERSIFYING. I have to admit, I thought Enron was finally going to do it. I thought all those stories of employees losing their stock-laden nest eggs at the same time they were losing their jobs would convince people that keeping too great a share of their portfolio in one stock—particularly company stock—was a dumb move. And yet, there I was on the day that Fannie Mae and Freddie Mac fell out of the sky hearing the same talk from employees and investors who had once again put all their eggs in one basket.

Why do we do this? Because we think we know better, particularly when we work for companies or are otherwise close to them. When our company stock is flailing, we don't sell because selling seems disloyal. When our company stock is soaring, we don't sell because it seems counterintuitive. Here's my rule: No more than 10 percent of your assets in any one stock, including company stock. If it becomes tough to toe that line because you work for a company that provides its 401(k) match in the form of company stock, diversify as soon as possible.

RAIDING A RETIREMENT ACCOUNT. A recent survey from Hewitt Associates shows we're still at it. When we leave jobs—which we now do an average twelve times over the course of a career—45 percent of us raid our retirement accounts. What we do with that money is unclear. We may pay down credit card debt. We may spend it on other needs or wants. What we are not doing is rolling it into an IRA or a new employer's plan or leaving it in our former employer's plan where it can continue to grow. Why do we do it? Sometimes we forget to roll the money over. Other times, the balance in the account seems so small and meaningless we are sure it will not amount to much over time. We are wrong.

Two thousand dollars invested tax-deferred earning a return of 8 percent will be worth $48,547 forty years down the road.

Five thousand dollars invested tax-deferred earning a return of 8 percent will be worth $54,679 thirty years down the road.

And $15,000 invested tax-deferred earning a return of 8 percent will be worth $73,902 twenty years down the road.

To make matters worse, by pulling the money out, we pay taxes and penalties of 30 percent—sometimes even more. That $2,000 becomes $1,400. That $5,000 becomes $3,500. That $15,000 shrivels to $10,000. Ask yourself "Is it worth it?" The answer is almost always no.

TRADING TOO MUCH. Do you think you trade like a pro? In one not-so-profitable way, you actually might. According to two recent academic studies, the typical mutual fund turns over 77 percent of its portfolio annually; the average individual investor, 75 percent. And each time we push the button, it seriously eats into our potential profits—not just because we might be buying or selling the wrong things at the wrong times, but because trading in and of itself gets expensive. Over the course of a lifetime, ignoring trading costs can zap your portfolio of more than $90,000, according to *Money* magazine.

How to avoid it? Stop trading except when you are rebalancing your portfolio twice a year. And fill your portfolio with index funds. Not only are they less costly to own, research has shown that only about 10 percent of active mutual fund managers have the ability to beat the markets. That may sound promising, but after the cost of investing with these managers is factored in, less than 1 percent still manage to come out ahead. When you buy index funds, you are buying the markets—and diversification—on the cheap. There is another alternative for people who know their own nature will prevent them from rebalancing on that twice-a-year schedule. (Trust me, if you have never been a reliable rebalancer in the past, there's no likelihood you will be in the future.) You should put your money into a target-date retirement fund that will be rebalanced for you as your retirement date approaches. Yes, target-date funds are more expensive than index funds. And you should choose carefully—some target-date funds are better than others. But at least you'll know you won't end up with a portfolio that is wildly out of whack.

BUYING THE NEXT HOT THING. You're at a cocktail party and your neighbor is regaling you with stories of how much money he made in oil in the last year. Or gold. And you get that familiar feeling—it's like kicking yourself from the inside. You would have, could have, should have bought some of those stocks yourself. And then a thought hits you: You could still buy them now. Wrong.

Our gut often tells us to follow the trend. To believe we're on to the next hot hand. The classic example is a coin toss. If you're flipping pennies and you've gotten heads fifteen times in a row, it's natural to believe that you're on a roll and you're going to keep getting heads. But in reality, one toss of the coin has no impact on the next, and the odds are fifty-fifty that you'll get tails every individual time. The same thing happens to investors. They get on a streak (or more likely just into a bull market) and start believing they are brilliant and can't go wrong. In fact, they can. And it can cost tens of thousands of dollars.

The key is to have a plan—a strategy—that determines what and when you buy, and what and when you sell. And remember, if you insist on trying to pick mutual funds rather than going the index route, the surest way to buy a fund that will consistently land in the top 25 percent of performers is to buy one with expenses in the bottom 25 percent. Look for the fund's expense ratio—the lower, the better.

IGNORING UNCLE SAM. Okay, so maybe the old guy with the gray beard is not as generous as we wish he was. But the government does give us many ways to invest in a tax-deferred or tax-free manner, and we don't take advantage of enough of them. Not enough of us max out our 401(k)s. Not enough of us make IRA contributions on a regular basis. Not enough of us kick money into 529 college savings accounts or health savings accounts where, again, the money can grow without having to worry that the long arm of the tax man is going to reach in there and take 15 to 20 percent. What else do we do wrong? We tend to sell winners rather than losers, which results in capital gains taxes. Selling losers, on the other hand, creates tax deductions. We also put the wrong investments—municipal bonds, for example—in tax-advantaged accounts like IRAs. Not only do they not need the tax advantages, but when we withdraw the money, interest that would otherwise be tax-exempt becomes fully taxable.

We make these mistakes because we don't think about taxes in the right way. That's not necessarily our fault. No one tells you how much they make in after-tax terms. (We should—we'd have a much better shot of living within our means. But that's a different problem not within the scope of this book.) Rather than thinking of reducing our tax bills, we should focus on increasing our after-tax incomes. That would lead us to ask questions about which assets should be sheltered and which should not, which should be sold and which should be kept to benefit the real bottom line. The solution lies in getting a hand with some tax planning—you can hire a person for this task or simply buy a tax-software program like Turbo Tax. And when you're evaluating mutual funds, pay attention to the after-tax numbers. Morningstar.com often runs after-tax, as well as pre-tax, performance comparisons.

Men, Women, and Money

Atop all these common mistakes, you have to deal with one more challenging arena: gender. When it comes to investing, men and women are different. Despite a great deal of reporting on the issue that encourages women to understand the necessity of equities for growth, women continue to be more risk averse. Look at the results of this question when the answers were broken down by gender.

Which describes the way you view the stock market?		
	Too risky for a large portion of my wealth	Worth the risk of a portion of my wealth because of the returns it can generate
Women	81 percent	19 percent
Men	40 percent	40 percent

That risk aversion is not a good thing. Because women take more breaks from the workforce, and earn only 81 cents for every dollar a man earns, women have less principal in retirement accounts to work with. Women need to take sufficient market risk to ensure that the balances in those accounts grow large enough to last through retirement. (Just, by the way, as men need to do.)

On the other hand, women—perhaps due to some of this same risk aversion—make trades in their accounts less frequently than men do. And that—according to the work of Terrance Odean and Brad Barber, professors of finance at the University of California at Berkeley and Davis, respectively, makes them better investors. Women tend to make fewer financial errors than men do, and the mistakes they do make are less serious.

Why are women more risk averse? You could argue that it's societal. Women have been included in the financial dialogue only recently and have long lacked enough information to make what they might think of as intelligent decisions in these areas. Also, with less money to their names, many women might feel they can simply not afford to lose any of it. But there's also a biological component. As Jason Zweig explained in *Your Money and Your Brain,* women are thought to be more right-brained than men are. And those people with greater right brain activity (specifically the right prefrontal cortex) tend to shy away from risk.

Making Your Money Grow

Man or woman, it comes down to this: You need a plan to prevent you from making any and all of these mistakes. You need to set goals, form a strategy, and start viewing the investing of your money as a means to an end—rather than an open-ended process of shoving as much as you can in your 401(k).

STEP ONE: Figure out how much you need to be putting away to satisfy your retirement goals. We dealt with that that on page 228.

STEP TWO: Decide how to allocate those assets you are putting away, which means determining how much of your money you want to put into stocks, how much into bonds, and how much into cash or cash substitutes. The average long-term return of the stock market since 1928 has bordered on 12 percent. But stocks, as we now well know, also represent the most risk. They have also gone up more than 30 percent (1995 and 1997) and down by more than 20 percent (2002 and 2008) in a single year. Bonds are not as risky as stocks, though they are by no means risk free. The average long-term return has been 5.4 percent, but in recent years (based on the performance of Vanguard's Total Bond Market Index Fund) they have gone up as much as 8.4 percent (2001) and as little as 2.4 percent (2005). Finally, there is cash or a cash substitute like a money market fund. Little to no risk in this category nets you a much smaller reward, historically around 3 percent. But you're not going to lose money.

Let's assume the goal is retirement. When you are young and you have many years—indeed many decades—until you will need to draw on that money, you can afford to take greater risk. If and when the market tumbles (and it will) you can use that opportunity to buy more shares so that when the market recovers (and it will) your nest egg will be worth substantially more. For that reason, the younger you are, the larger the share of your portfolio you'll want to keep in stocks. Not only are bonds less risky than stocks, but they tend to move in the opposite direction of stocks, though this is not set in stone. If you have a year when your stocks do poorly, having money in bonds will generally cushion your returns. You may still lose money overall, but you won't lose as much. Similarly, during a year when the market is going gangbusters, allocating some of your assets to bonds typically means your returns won't grow as fat as they might if your entire nest egg is in stocks.

Professional mutual fund managers try to beat the markets by moving in and out of stocks and bonds—indeed, in and out of particular sectors of stocks and bonds, or in and out of individual stock and bond issues—based on their forecasts of which will do particularly well, and when. The majority—as I said earlier—fail at their attempts. The fact that they fail so often has led me and many of the financial experts I respect to the following conclusion: Why even try to beat the market?

Instead of trying to pick stocks or bonds or sectors or funds, buy index funds. They're cheap. They're easy. And you can cover your bases with three index funds: a total stock market index fund (domestic), a total bond market index fund, and an international stock-market index fund. To find a good one with low fees, go to Morningstar.com.

How to Allocate Your Assets

What do you get by allocating your assets into these three funds? The whole enchilada. The total stock market index fund buys you large caps and small caps, growth and value. The bond market fund does essentially the same thing. And the international fund gives you access to a broad array of international stocks in one portfolio. How do you decide how much to put in each?

It depends on your age (and how close you are to retirement) and your risk tolerance—and the former should largely determine the latter.

EARLY IN YOUR CAREER (TWENTIES TO THIRTIES)
50 percent Total Stock Index Fund

20 percent International Stock Index Fund

20 percent Total Bond Market Index Fund

10 percent Cash or Money Market Fund

MIDCAREER (FORTIES TO FIFTIES)
45 percent Total Stock Index Fund

15 percent International Stock Index Fund

30 percent Total Bond Market Index Fund

10 percent Cash or Money Market Fund

LATE CAREER, EARLY RETIREMENT (SIXTIES TO SEVENTIES)
35 percent Total Stock Index Fund

10 percent International Stock Index Fund

40 percent Total Bond Market Index Fund

15 percent Cash or Money Market Fund

RETIREMENT (EIGHTY AND OLDER)
25 percent Total Stock Index Fund

5 percent International Stock Index Fund

40 percent Total Bond Market Index Fund

30 percent Cash or Money Market Fund

The only thing required of you if you choose to go this route is maintenance. Twice a year—on your birthday and half birthday, let's say, or right around Christmas and the fourth of July—you need to take a look at your accounts. If stocks have gone on a tear, you may need to sell some of your stock fund and buy some shares of your bond fund to right your asset allocations. If bonds have had a tremendous run, you may need to sell some shares of your bond fund and buy some of your stock fund in order to do the same.

Let me acknowledge there have been years in which I knew that life had gotten so busy I was not going to get around to doing even that basic rebalancing. (Young children will do that to you.) If you're having a year or two or even a decade like that, then ignore the advice about indexing and put your money into a target-date retirement mutual fund instead. Also called lifecycle funds, these mutual funds—which have names like the 2030 fund or 2035 fund—rebalance themselves with an eye toward retirement for the year in their names. They take fewer and fewer risks as they close in on those dates so that if the market tanks right before you retire, you should be protected. About half of all retirement plans have them right now, according to research from the AARP—but that number is growing fast.

Allot 5 to 10 Percent of Your Money to "Play"

There will come a time when you are reading the newspaper or watching television and you'll hear about some new widget or gadget or medical technology or fashion that you think is drop-dead brilliant. Or your neighbor will tell you of her plans for a new business that you think is right on target. Or you'll have the opportunity to get some shares of stock at the friends and family price. And you'll think: I want to put some money there.

Well, I think everyone should have the opportunity to speculate once in a while . . . with 5 to 10 percent of their money. Just don't allow yourself to believe it's anything other than what it is, a high-risk/high-reward proposition. If it pays off you'll be sitting pretty. If it doesn't, allow yourself to enjoy the ride knowing that it won't harm your ability to retire, send your kids to college, or meet any of your other financial goals.

HOW ABOUT INVESTING IN A BUSINESS OF YOUR OWN?

No doubt about it, one way individuals make their way to wealth is by starting a successful business. It may not be the first business, the second business, or the ninth business that hits pay dirt, but our research shows that it's a leading way to wealth.

Would you describe yourself as a business owner?

	Yes
Wealthy	21 percent
Financially comfortable	13 percent
Paycheck-to-paychecks	12 percent
Further-in-debtors	11 percent

To get rich this way, you need not only the desire—you need the entrepreneurial mind-set. When Frederick Crane of Northeastern University interviews his business school students, 85 percent say they want to start their own businesses. Less than 10 percent of them, he reports, will actually do it.

What holds them back? Risk. The fact that they're putting their money, their time, their ego—and quite often their family's security—on the line. But Crane has learned over the years that most successful entrepreneurs don't take the fifty-fifty gamble. Entrepreneurs take a particular kind of calculated risk. They are aware of their personal limitations so they look for their own weaknesses and hire people who can fill those gaps.

Think of an entrepreneurial risk as a football game. Let's say it's fourth down and three. Most teams would punt. But if you have three yards to go and are confident in your rushing game, it's not as big a risk for you to try to make the first down as it would be for a team that has a lousy rushing game. Entrepreneurs don't consider business ownership as risky as the rest of the population does. They view risk as something they should lessen if possible, often by using other people's money if they can get it. From the point of view of the objective probability of success, yes it's risky, but from their personal context, it's not as risky as it might be to someone else.

Getting Some Help

Look, if you were worried about your heart, marriage, or career, you'd very likely find someone—a cardiologist, therapist, or coach—to help you. A good financial adviser can, at the least, prevent you from doing yourself harm. There are times in our lives when we need someone else who will let us bounce ideas off them. If left to our own devices, we are often too susceptible to our own biases and bad ideas. The wealthy understand this. More than six out of ten of them have used financial advisers to help them find their way.

Have you ever worked with a financial advisor?	
	Yes
Wealthy	61 percent
Financially comfortable	45 percent
Paycheck-to-paychecks	21 percent
Further-in-debtors	15 percent

So how do you find a financial adviser to help you? I prefer to start by asking colleagues (who are likely in a similar financial situation or at least in the same industry) for recommendations. Generate a short list of names and set up informational interviews with three or four candidates. Find out what that financial adviser would recommend to a person in your situation. Make sure you understand how this person will be paid and how much this relationship will cost you over a year's time. Focus on the adviser's recommendations for how much risk you should be taking with your investments. Ask for references—*and check them.* And ask to see a plan your adviser has prepared for someone else (with no names or identifying details, of course). Finally, make a gut call. It is imperative that you're able to have an open and honest conversation with whomever you hire. If you are not comfortable disclosing past financial mistakes with this person, he or she is not the right financial adviser for you, no matter how highly recommended they are.

What if you can't gather enough recommendations to create a short list? The following are websites of prominent financial planning organizations. Each has a locator service.

- FPAnet.org: The website of the Financial Planning Association, the largest organization of financial advisers.
- NAPFA.org: The website of the National Association of Personal Financial Advisors, an organization for fee-only financial advisers.
- Garrettplanningnetwork.com: A website of the Garrett Planning Network, which is made up of fee-only financial advisers, many of whom are willing to work by the hour.

Once All the Pieces Are in Place: Hands Off

You'll be much better suited to investing (and come to think of it, to most other things in life) if you can get over the impulse to try to nail it. Years of research by Terrance Odean, a finance professor at the University of California at Berkeley, show that individual investors tend to do themselves far more harm than good when they muck with their portfolios.

On average, if they buy one stock and sell another, the one they sell goes on to do better than the one they buy. And those who try to time the market do worse, on average, than those who don't.

Odean's recommendation: Let's not and say we did. "My advice is simply not to try to time the market. The average investor should buy well-diversified mutual funds that are fairly low-cost," he explains. So how do you overcome the urge to, for lack of a better word, fiddle?

By controlling the things you can control.

I wrote the majority of this book in 2008, which—as years in the market go—was tumultuous. Housing fell out of the sky. Oil rose into the stratosphere. We saw gold tip $1,000 an ounce. And through it all investors—many of them, at least—shook in their boots. A few Wall

Streeters in my circle (smart people, I promise) set up a corner in their basements and started stockpiling food. I started to wish there was some über-psychiatrist who could put the market on a little Prozac.

Unfortunately, neither my wishful thinking nor anybody else's contained the cure. Instead, I've learned, feeling better is a matter of controlling the things I can control: my own behavior as well as the turbulence in my own mind. If you'd like to follow along with me:

ACKNOWLEDGE THAT YOU'RE SCARED. Actually get out a piece of paper and write your concerns down. Then you can look at your list and ask, "How realistic are these fears?" In my case, at the top of the list is the high probability I bought my home at the tippy-top of the market then plowed in more renovation dollars than I can ever hope to recoup. How realistic is that? If I had to sell today, I'd be out six figures. But I also know that no loss is real until you actually have to take it—and I'm not planning on moving for a very long time.

DON'T BUY SOMETHING. When you read in the newspaper or see some analyst on TV shouting about how the housing market is crashing or that your stocks are worthless, somewhere in the recesses of your mind you know this doesn't have anything to do with rational economics, explains Robert Meyer, chairman of the marketing department at the Wharton School of the University of Pennsylvania. "They're talking about a home you're not planning on selling anytime soon, and retirement is years in the future. You're not really becoming poor—you're just feeling like you are." He suggests giving yourself a momentary dose of wealth. How? By withholding a discretionary purchase. Don't buy the shoes. Don't upgrade the iPod. "The function of this little act of prudence is much more psychological than real. It's not going to make you that much better off in retirement. But it gives you the mental sensation of having more money again."

SAVE MORE. If that doesn't do the trick, up the ante and actually make the effort to save a little more money every day. This goes back to the notion that saving can be very healing. I, for one, get a surge of pleasure when I check my 529 account balances online and see that—despite the fact that the returns haven't been stellar—my monthly contributions keep the balances moving in the right direction.

TAME YOUR SURROUNDINGS. Controlling your environment creates a sense of peace and calm. To start—stop acquiring. Then purge anything that doesn't help you create the life you want. Focus on the quality of the items, not the quantity of the items. You'll see, you'll feel calmer with less.

FINALLY, FIGHT YOUR KNEE-JERK REACTIONS. This is where having a financial plan (or at the very least some goals) comes in very handy. When you are feeling like you want to jump into or out of the market, you have the advantage of being able to turn to your plan and touch base with reality. Action, experts say, is also a good antidote to the urge to do something dangerous. Get up and away from the phone or computer, and take a walk instead. And if you have an adviser, this is a good time to check in. If you don't have one, this is an excellent time to find one. (And when you do decide on one, go in with the list of fears you made earlier. Anxiety can make you less coherent and less articulate. Having your list in writing is insurance you won't leave the session and then have one V8 moment after another.)

Why Getting Older Is Not a Bad Thing, Part III

In my family, there is story after story about my father's father, Abe, who in his youth was very much a my-way-or-the-highway kind of guy. Dinner had to be on the table at six. His shirts—and boxer shorts—ironed just so. And he was Jewish, just this side of Orthodox, which meant keeping a kosher home and using no electricity on Shabbat.

Abe lived to be ninety-eight. We liked to say that as he aged, he mellowed. He made friends with my dog, who would in earlier years have been considered a nuisance. He gave up on the concept of ironed shorts. He enjoyed eating Chinese out—though he opted for the shrimp instead of the chicken because the chicken might be pork.

Turns out this is what happens to our brains as they age. They mellow. We no longer feel fear as strongly, and that makes us better investors, workers, employers, and business owners. Why? Because it gives us the fortitude to withstand swings in the markets, our bosses' moods, and our companies' ups and downs. It's not all good. Some of the skepticism that marks younger, more cynical individuals is helpful in avoiding scams and other bad ideas.

The recommendation: Once you—or your parents—are staring seventy in the face, it's time to bring a financial professional into the picture. This person can provide the sort of sanity check you or your parent once might have been able to handle themselves. Of course, you could fill this role for your parent—provided they are among those parents who are willing to take financial advice from their offspring (and not all are).

Exercise: Keep an Investing Journal

We make mistakes with our money when we allow emotion to overwhelm rationality. It's true with shopping. It may be even truer with investing. This exercise was developed to help you deal with feelings that may be overshadowing certain facts.

WHEN YOU PICK A PARTICULAR INVESTMENT, MAKE YOURSELF ANSWER THIS QUESTION.

WHY AM I BUYING THIS STOCK / BOND / FUND / INVESTMENT AT THIS TIME?

I EXPECT THAT IT WILL RETURN _____ PERCENT ANNUALLY.

I BELIEVE I WILL SELL IT WHEN _____.

Then, when you are inclined to get out, go back and look at the argument you laid out the first time around. You'll get a sense of whether you're simply selling because the investment (or the market as a whole) has been on a roller coaster or for a more fundamental reason. You'll start to see patterns in your own tendencies to react—or even overreact. And that, like all of these exercises you adopt, will make more of a difference than you know.

AFTERWORD

Was 2008 a good time to write this book? That was a notion my editor and I debated as we got page proofs back in October, right after the market hit its worst week in many, many years.

In fact, I have come to believe that it was the perfect time. The people whose stories I've included were, for the most part, in their fifties and sixties at the time of their interviews. They had parents who had lived through the Depression, and consequently had enforced dinner-table lessons about the sorts of old-fashioned values that turned out to embody The Difference: Work hard, save every day, when life kicks you to the curb find a way to get right back up again. Practice, practice, practice.

For me, researching and writing *The Difference* has been a transformative experience. I now understand more about my own behavior, my own attitudes, and my own success than I did a year ago. *The Difference* has provided me with a filter to process questions about my money, my career, and my life. And I believe I am stronger—in all of those capacities—as a result.

I hope that you will find *The Difference* helps you in many of those same ways—and that you'll share your experiences with me. Please visit me at JeanChatzky.com. There, you can ask me questions, share your successes and frustrations, and tell me about your quest for The Difference. I look forward to continuing this journey together.

Jean Chatzky

INDEX

ABOUT THE AUTHOR

JEAN CHATZKY, award-winning journalist, bestselling author, and sought-after motivational speaker, has created a global platform that is making significant strides to help millions of men and women battle an epidemic with a devastating impact—debt. Jean is the financial editor for NBC's *Today*, a contributing editor for *More Magazine*, a columnist for the New York *Daily News*, and a contributor to *The Oprah Winfrey Show*. She also hosts a daily show on the Oprah & Friends channel, exclusively on Sirius XM Radio.

She is the author of numerous books, including *Pay It Down!: From Debt to Wealth on $10 a Day*, a *New York Times* and *Business-Week* bestseller, as well as *Make Money, Not Excuses*, a *Wall Street Journal* and *New York Times* bestseller.

Jean has been recognized as as an exceptional journalist. She received the Clarion Award for her magazine columns from the Association for Women in Communications, her radio show received a Gracie Award from American Women in Radio and Television, and she has been nominated twice for National Magazine Awards and was named one of the country's best magazine columnists by the *Chicago Tribune*.

In addition to her professional work, Jean is on the March of

Dimes advisory council, lends her support and expertise to women's services groups, and is on the board of the Nora Magid Mentorship Prize at the University of Pennsylvania, which helps journalism students get a head start in the field. She is also on the Communications Committee for the University of Pennsylvania.

Jean lives with her family in Westchester, New York.

Also by Jean Chatzky

The essential companion to Jean Chatzky's The Difference

This companion journal takes the writing and planning exercises crafted and recommended in *The Difference* and provides interactive entry pages for plotting out your life goals and your financial ones.

(Jean Chatzky's research indicates that journaling is one of the most common habits of the self-made wealthy.)

THE DIFFERENCE WEALTH-BUILDING JOURNAL
Discover How You Can Prosper in Even the Toughest Times
$14.95 paper (Canada: $16.95)
978-0-307-45286-3

Get Rich, Don't Bitch

In *Make Money, Not Excuses,* Jean Chatzky breaks down the scariest parts of dealing with money—from investing in stocks to saving for your retirement—and makes them practical, easy, empowering, and, yes, even enjoyable.

MAKE MONEY, NOT EXCUSES
Wake Up, Take Charge, and Overcome Your Financial Fears Forever
$13.95 paper (Canada: $15.95)
978-0-307-34153-2

Available wherever books are sold